PRAISE FOR THE *IMPACTER*

"Whether you are striving for an NBA championship ofr closing your next deal, the leadership lessons of The Impacter will transform the way you work and live."

—**Pat Williams**, Co-Founder, Orlando Magic

"This clever parable brings to the forefront many key fundamentals for strong leadership and motivation. It inspires you to do more and be more through its creativity and thoughtfulness."

—**Dr. Nido Qubein**, President, High Point University
Chairman, Great Harvest Bread Co.

"A wonderful parable that will speak directly to your soul in an inspiring and profound way. It's a joy to read, contains loads of *aha* moments and is a perfect tool for helping anyone integrate their faith and business purpose. This book will both delight you and cause you to really think!"

—**Jason Jennings**, *New York Times* Best-selling Author of *It's Not The Big That Eat The Small–It's The Fast That Eat The Slow, Less Is More, Think BIG–Act Small, Hit The Ground Running,* and *The Reinventors*

"Jim has packed so much useful, insightful and practical wisdom into a great story that will help you get focused or refocused on what is important both in your business and personal life!"
—**Todd Hopkins**, Founder & CEO of Office Pride Commercial Cleaning Services, international best-selling author

"Dr. Jim, why can't you write something boring and old school...something that doesn't have me running around the office with flip charts and dreams of webinars? I was having a perfectly ordinary week, and here you come with your "Impacter" to get me all stirred up...ought to be a law against it!! Fantastic book."
—**Shane Satterfield**, Southeast Region Vice President, Marketplace Chaplains USA

"*The Impacter* is a great read. The four virtues of Character, Competence, Courage and Commitment spelled out in this book are virtues that every Bible based organization should cherish and revolve around."
—**Jim Brangenberg**, Regional Manager, Platinum Information Services, Inc.

"If you struggle with how to erase the line between faith and work, you will devour this book. This allegory instructs the soul and feeds the spirit in an entertaining, profound way. I cannot wait to share it with our entire leadership team."

—**Jim Gates**, Brand Manager, Quality Filters, Inc.

"Your parable is fascinating. Purpose and calling must undergird positive and lasting (eternal) outcomes."

—**Win Hallett**, President, Mobile Area Chamber of Commerce

THE
IMPACTER

A PARABLE ON
TRANSFORMATIONAL LEADERSHIP

DR. JIM HARRIS

HIGH BRIDGE BOOKS
HOUSTON

The Impacter
by Dr. Jim Harris

© 2015 by Dr. Jim Harris

Second edition.

High Bridge Books titles may be purchased in bulk for educational, business, fund-raising, or sales promotional use. For information please contact High Bridge Books via www.HighBridgeBooks.com/contact.

Published in Houston, Texas by High Bridge Books

Cover design by Matt Arnold

Printed in the United States of America

ISBN (Paperback): 978-1-940024-45-5
ISBN (eBook): 978-1-940024-46-2

OTHER BOOKS BY DR. JIM HARRIS

Beyond Motivation

Getting Employees to Fall in Love with your Company

Finding & Keeping Great Employees (with Joan Brannick)

Management Excellence

Corporate Excellence

Management Excellent for Pastors

Managing@NetSpeed

Heartpower

The Employee Connection

Management 24/7

Culture 24/7

Leadership 24/7

Our Unfair Advantage: Unleash the Power of the
Holy Spirit in Your Business

CONTENTS

ACKNOWLEDGEMENTS

First and foremost, this book is dedicated to my Lord and Savior, Jesus Christ. I truly desire for Him to receive whatever glory and honor this book may bring.

To my wife, Brenda, and my son, Jason. May God mold me into the husband and father you both deserve.

To Deborah Burdick, whose relentless and passionate editing transformed my original sloppy manuscript into a professional book.

To the dozens of friends, clients, and colleagues whose ideas, feedback, and insights I blended into this story. You are too many to name, yet you know who you are.

"Glorify the Lord with me. Let us exalt His name together." Psalm 34:3

INTRODUCTION

In every life we meet unique individuals who impact who we are, what we think, what we believe, and where we end up, both in this life and beyond. I call these people "Impacters."

This book is my first and best effort to tell the story of such a person, a man who impacts those around him in timeless ways.

The characters are based upon people I have worked alongside, consulted with, and observed in my business career. My hope is that many of them are as familiar to you as they are to me.

I also hope their insights, challenges, and conclusions both inspire and potentially transform your life.

This is a work of fiction. Any resemblance to a real company or real people is totally unavoidable!

Chapter 1

THE REPORTER

I'm Tony Sullivan. I've been a senior reporter at Lens Shift magazine for the past seven years. Just celebrated my 50th birthday.

Before you read this story, you need to hear mine. You'll see why after you finish this book.

Following a brief stint after college as a struggling magician and author, I landed at a big firm that needed someone to produce internal training videos and other in-house corporate communications. Thought, "Why not?" I could do this as my day job and still dabble with my "magic" at night. Then was approached by the VP of Marketing about being promoted to public relations manager. Took it. And that began my fast-track journey into the wonderful world of corporate communications.

I grew to like and even thrive on the nomadic lifestyle in Fortune 500 firms. My LinkedIn resume expanded to include all my experience leading media and public relations departments inside a broad spectrum of multi- billon dollar retail, entertainment, and beverage conglomerates.

I worked with companies that expanded and contracted, downsized and right sized, reengineered and reorganized, and centralized and decentralized. For two decades I lived virtually every "flavor of the month" management fad.

At the ripe old age of 43, I'd had enough of the Fortune 500 insider grind, including endless infighting and bureaucracy, budget battles, turf wars, and worst of all, lack of scruples and integrity throughout the firms. I decided to take the leap and finally pursue my passion–writing as a freelancer about the very same firms that once employed me. I'd seen enough of the shenanigans and the talk-it-but-don't-walk-it crowd to make me more than a little cynical about covering yet another of "today's business success stories."

Why the cynicism? Because I used to be a part of "The Game" of masterfully manipulating the right amount of the latest corporate jargon gleaned from the never-ending parade of business gurus paid to speak at annual meetings to make it sound like we were doing all the right things. I could weave a verbal and visual story well enough to make any company into the next great darling of the media.

I'd been freelancing for several years when Bart Simons, managing editor of Lens Shift magazine, offered me a job. I accepted immediately. When he hired me, I had just enough business writing experience to keep up with the need-it-done-now world of publishing, but more important to Bart, I had enough corporate insider experience to see beyond the public relations hype and bogus nonsense. I knew the story wasn't what companies were saying about themselves.

Since becoming an investigative reporter for Lens Shift, I've uncovered and exposed countless profit-hungry, greedy, heartless, manipulative businesses whose only desire is to maximize their net worth and destroy their competition, whether inside or outside their firms.

Like everyone else, I've read and heard about the business scandals coming to light around the world. From Ponzi schemes to billions of investment dollars that suddenly disappeared, we've all come to expect the worst from businesses and their owners. It's now my job to find them, write about them, and make them look...well...not good.

Scandal sells.

Yes, my highly developed, controlled cynicism of most things corporate is immovable, unshakable, and typically 100% reliable. It's how I make my living, after all. I've continued to let it guide me like a bloodhound on the trail.

That's before I met Joe Grayson and his team.

Chapter 2

THE ASSIGNMENT

For more than 80 years, Lens Shift magazine has covered virtually every aspect of business. From breaking trends to breakthrough technology to corporate breakups, Lens Shift has aggressively pursued news-making business ventures and the people who lead them.

Many of our hardest-hitting stories deal with the underside of business, taking apart companies and executives that go rogue. Lens Shift has an uncanny knack for uncovering the roses among the thorns just before they bloom. Our investigative reporters have broken the stories and led the news on Wal-Mart, Southwest Airlines, Zappos, and Google before those companies became household names and, in the case of Google, even a household verb.

Lately, Lens Shift has broadened its focus to include not only the country's fastest-growing and most profitable companies, but also those best embodying what future firms must be and do to stay profitable and relevant.

No small task.

This morning, Bart Simons, our managing editor, has called me into his office to give me an assignment where the stakes could not be higher.

For the last several years, digital media has steadily eroded our print edition subscription base. Newsstand and home circulation sales have dropped drastically. Our digital version is getting some initial traction, but it's far from recouping the income lost from dropped subscriptions and advertising revenues.

One issue of our monthly publication stands out among the others. Typically, the sale of this single "Spotlight" issue determines the financial pulse rate and profitability of the publication, and our firm, for the coming year.

Over the past year, our operating budget has been slashed 23%. We've laid off 15 full-time staff members. Without an immediate infusion of revenue, Bart will be forced to send more people packing, slice deeper into our already razor-thin budgets, and consider the painful possibility of a potential sale or dissolution of the print publishing division.

Compounding the pressure, Bart has only two years until full retirement. He's not the only one around here that hopes he makes it. He's paid his dues and more than deserves it. Bart has worked incredibly hard over the past 15 years to build one of the best business magazines in the country. Everyone here, including the Board of Directors, recognizes his incredible skills and passion for doing his best, and his relentless push to make everyone around him the best, too. [We all admire him and enjoy working for him.]

We all feel the pressure he's under. All we need to do is glance at the deepening bags under his eyes and observe the ever-present cup of coffee in his hand as he makes his rounds.

Approaching Bart's office, I'm greeted by Liz Morgan, his executive assistant, already on duty at her desk outside his door and ready to help wherever needed. That's her style. Liz is undoubtedly the best executive assistant Bart's ever had–thorough, efficient, reliable, and positive. There's something very special about Liz, but even for a group of writers, it eludes definition.

"Good morning, Tony," Liz calls out cheerfully. "He's expecting you–just go on in."

This meeting, and this assignment, isn't just a routine story for a regular monthly issue. It's The Story, the one all the staff reporters subtly angle to get. And one of the most important decisions a managing editor makes is assigning the right reporter to each story. Sometimes it's intuition, but most often it's experience that dictates the choice.

Bart has a host of other talent at his disposal. Susan Ford is a fantastic researcher and a bulldog of a reporter. She's been with Lens Shift for six years. Imagine a polished female version of

Mike Wallace with legendary instincts and killer professional credentials. Her attention to detail and determination to do almost anything to get the story has earned her the respect of colleagues and rivals alike.

Carmelo Costales is a rising superstar in business news reporting. He's a bright, tireless worker with a top-notch education from Cornell and street smarts from growing up in southwest Houston. He gives every story a pungent, real-world aroma–his stories resonate with powerful intensity.

Bill Carter is the pro's pro. He's the senior reporter at Lens Shift, and he cut his teeth covering business stories in the Nixon administration in the early 1970's. He's reported on dozens of scandals, trends, break ups, hot companies, and financial matters. A gifted writer and analyst, Bill is highly respected inside and outside our circle.

Bart wastes no time on small talk.

"Tony, this assignment is yours," he says in his typical blunt editor's manner. "This year's pick is Grayson Human Resources. Get with Liz to set up your travel to Grayson. They're in Bowling Green, Kentucky. Their CEO, Joe Grayson, has been briefed that you'll be coming. Get on his schedule and then let Liz know all the details."

Turning his attention to the papers on his desk, Bart glances up at me over his reading glasses. "First draft due by next Thursday. If you need any support from anyone here, go to them directly. They know this is priority one, and you don't need my approval." He calls out to Liz, just outside his door. "Liz, send out a short email to that effect–Tony has the authority to ask anyone for help on this assignment, and if contacted, they're to respond same day. " He glanced back at me. "Any questions, Tony?"

I shake my head, my mind already beginning to whirl and plan. "No Bart. I know how important this assignment is. We need to hit a home run. Thanks for this opportunity. I won't let you down."

Bart nods. "I know that, Tony. You never have and I know you'll give it your best. Keep me posted on your progress, and call me for anything you need." He glances at his phone, already on to the next thing. "Now, get to work."

I excuse myself and leave the office, already deep in thought. Next Thursday! That's only eight days away. Typical deadlines on lead stories allow at least three weeks of development time, and the Spotlight story normally gets five weeks.

Now the pressure is on. I fervently hope I can come through, not only for the company, but for myself, too. I love my work, and love working for Lens Shift. But regardless of how any of us feel about the company, our jobs are always on the line.

At 50 years old and in this economy, I sure don't want to try to find another job in journalism. Might as well go back to being a struggling magician.

Banishing that unpleasant prospect, I settle behind my desk, nudge my computer mouse, and Google Grayson HR.

Chapter 3

FIRST IMPRESSIONS

B owling Green, Kentucky is a beautiful mid-sized college town 60 miles north of Nashville, just 20 miles north of the central Tennessee state border. It's known as much for its rich history, from Daniel Boone settlements to Civil War battles, as it is for having the tallest building in southern Kentucky. Pierce-Ford Tower is a 27-floor dormitory on the south side of the campus of Western Kentucky University.

How would I know about Pierce-Ford Tower? I was a freshman there in 1971 when it first opened as an all-male dormitory, and my room was on the seventh floor room facing north toward "The Hill." I wore myself out as a freshman walking up that hill for my late afternoon English classes, and learned firsthand why they are nicknamed "The Hilltoppers."

The entire area surrounding Bowling Green has exploded with growth over the past 20 years, becoming home to the international headquarters of Fruit of the Loom, a long-time resident, and welcoming the relatively new and sprawling General Motors Corvette assembly plant and museum, both on the east side of town close to I-65. Just ask the locals about the amount of traffic along the Scottsville Road corridor running east and west from I-65 and you'll get an earful about the not-so-great side of growth.

*****

Pulling my rental car into an "Our Guests" parking space close to Grayson HR's front entrance, I was reminded of the old adage, "First impressions are lasting impressions." I don't necessarily believe that. In most successful businesses, the first impression is usually good. My job is to dig for the reality behind that first impression; that's what I'm paid to uncover and expose. In my experience, in business and in life, things are not usually what they seem…at first.

I glanced quickly over the neatly manicured landscape, the simple, inviting entrance, and the calm façade typically found outside most professional office buildings. This one, I noted, was especially well kept.

The clean, contemporary architecture of the Grayson building made it stand out from most general office buildings. With an entrance of beautiful tile and glass walls that wrapped around the main entrance, I could actually see into the reception area, to the conference room just to the left of the entrance, and into an employee and guest seating area with large, buttery soft leather couches, bright accent pillows, and elegantly designed coffee tables.

My outsider's view of the building and grounds was positive, and I came away impressed. Would the interior meet the same high standards?

I grabbed my well-worn canvas satchel holding my laptop as well as the ever-present assortment of reporter's notebooks and pens. After locking the rental car, I headed up the walk toward the building's main entrance, where I noted the absence of any kind of keypad or controlled entry. The door opened easily and I stepped inside.

Before the door closed behind me, I heard a friendly voice say, "Welcome to Grayson HR. I'm Francis. Might you be Mr. Sullivan?" A pleasant-faced woman sat at a small reception desk, beaming at me over the top of a pair of reading glasses. Behind her, on a computer monitor, a screen saver of photos paraded across the screen. Since many of the subjects had the woman's same irrepressible red curls and dimpled smile, I guessed they were her family.

"Yes, that's me. Was it that easy to tell?"

"Well, Mr. Sullivan, everyone here knows about your visit, and we're thrilled to be the subject of your story." Her dimples deepened. "And truth is, not that many people around here walk into our offices with a bag that has "Lens Shift Magazine" on it."

"You've got the makings of a great investigative journalist."

Francis' smile broadened.

"Oh no, thank you, but I appreciate the compliment. Mr. Grayson is expecting you. Let me ring his office and let him know you're here."

As she dialed the number, I glanced at her name plate neatly angled on the top of her desk with the inscription, "Francis Green–Director of First Impressions." I've been to plenty of companies that, after listening to a motivational speaker, attending a seminar, or reading a book, suddenly "get religion" and change job titles of folks to something cool and hip, thinking that's how to take their firm to a higher level. Was Grayson one of them?

But today, with my first impression of Francis, I wondered if this company really did grasp the concept of "first impressions."

"Mr. Grayson will be right out," Francis said, pressing a button on her phone. "Can I get you some water, coffee, juice, or something else?" I shook my head.

"No, thank you. I just finished breakfast at the hotel. I'm fine."

Before I had time to sit down in the reception area, a tall, energetic man walked briskly into Francis' area. His khaki pants were crisply pressed, the stripes on his red and white tie reflected his loyalty to Western Kentucky University, and the sleeves on his Oxford shirt were rolled up, indicating a readiness for hands-on work. With a big, warm smile that spread into his blue eyes, he extended his right hand and said, "I'm Joe Grayson. Welcome to our family."

What? You MUST be kidding me! Our family?

I returned his smile and found his handshake equally warm and welcoming. If I didn't know better, I mused, this guy acted like he could hardly wait to meet me. Me? A reporter? After we exchanged greetings, Joe turned to Francis and asked, "Now, you've taken good care of Tony so far, right, Francis?" His knowing smile and gentle tone conveyed to us his certainty of the same.

"Oh, yes sir. But why don't you ask Mr. Sullivan himself?" Francis responded.

Seeing an opportunity, I spoke up. "Francis is extremely cordial and accommodating," I said. "She represents Grayson HR very well. Maybe she should be the featured employee in the article?"

With a big, appreciative grin and a warm laugh, Joe said, "You're absolutely right. Francis, let's make you the star of this article. Tony, have you got your camera with you today?"

"Oh no you don't, gentlemen," Francis jokingly interjected. "Don't even think of taking my picture today! Wait until next Thursday when I get my hair done. Then, maybe."

"OK then, no pictures today," Joe said easily. He extended a hand toward a doorway. "Tony, let's go to my office."

Chapter 4

UNDER THE HOOD

Passing through the doorway, my first glimpse of the general office environment of Grayson HR was, I must say, positive. Modern aluminum and opaque glass screens separated neatly arranged workspaces, affording some measure of privacy while still allowing face-to-face conversations and easy circulation. The workspaces themselves were clean and thoughtfully organized, with what looked to be plenty of storage.

Moving easily throughout the office, Joe introduced me to several Grayson HR staff members from the payroll, underwriting, business development, safety, and human resources departments. Every person was pleasant, cheerful, and respectful.

I've seen all this before, I mused. Everybody putting their best foot forward, And anyway, I was with the boss man!

Joe's office was in the back of the general work area. A tall set of contemporary birch doors opened into a small but functional executive office. Two large computer monitors—as expected. Desk and credenza—check. Herman Miller chair—not un-usual. However, I was struck by the panoramic window wall, the high ceilings, the slowing rotating ceiling fan with a Pueblo-style light fixture, the soft baseball-glove leather sofa for guests, and the collection of trophy animal heads hanging on the wall. Behind the animals, a floor to ceiling wall graphic made me feel as if I'd stepped into the southwestern hill and desert country.

"You enjoy hunting," I commented.

"Yes, I do," Joe said, his eyes brightening. Do you do any hunting?"

"Only on the golf course," I said.

Joe laughed and admitted, "Me too. In fact, I do some of my best hunting in the woods next to the fairway I just missed."

He invited me to take a seat and offered me something to drink.

"Water would be great, if you have it," I said. Joe reached into a small refrigerator near the sitting area, extracted two cold bottles of water labeled with the Grayson logo, and set them on cocktail napkins on a table in front of me.

"Will this work for your laptop?" he asked, pulling a small wheeled table forward. I noted his attentiveness to the needs of his visitors as I quickly set up my laptop and recording equipment.

Ready with my normal spiel…"You know, Joe, Lens Shift has decided to feature your firm in its "Spotlight" article this year. How does it feel to be on the verge of instant celebrity status?

I paused, expecting the usual well-rehearsed false humility. After all, he knew why I was here. No surprises. But what Joe said after a moment's silence surprised me.

"Tony, as you get to know us and check us out under the hood, you'll learn we are indeed a little different than what I imagine you typically see. I subscribe to Lens Shift. I've read your work and I like what I see in your writing. You take a hard-nosed, no-nonsense approach to the firms you cover. I admire that. I really do. I expect you to do exactly the same during your visit with us."

Joe settled back in his chair and pressed his fingertips together. His expression became more serious.

"But I'll tell you up front that the thought of 'instant celebrity' and 'fame' run counter to who we are and how we approach business at Grayson HR. You'll see this soon enough. All I ask of you in this article is that you be fair and objective. Where we have holes, I expect you to expose them. And trust me, we do. Where we have strengths and convictions, I ask you to report them candidly and accurately. "

Somewhat taken aback by Joe's approach, I listened intently as he continued.

"I do not expect this to be a fluff piece, nor do I expect this to be a seek-and-destroy piece. I know your magazine's financial footprint. Anyone can read your disclosures in the print version every week and see how important this issue is to you, your team, and your financials. And I must admit, of all your fellow reporters, I was very pleased they chose you to write this story."

Something about Joe's candor, openness, honesty, and directness was at once refreshing and disarming.

"Joe," I replied, leaning forward, "I give you my word that I will do exactly what you have asked me to do. I'll write a totally candid, honest and accurate piece."

"I appreciate that, Tony," Joe said, his eyes crinkling with a smile. "People's word means a lot around here to us. In fact, I can see already that you could potentially be a good fit for Grayson HR. You seem to possess the same basic virtues we embrace."

Virtues? Did I hear that right?

Oh no, here we go again, I thought. Another "fluffy" firm trying to impress the outsider with their "holier than thou" values, credos, standards, foundations, or in this case, virtues.

Corporate crap alert duly noted, I thought with a twinge of regret. I'd hoped Grayson HR wouldn't fall prey to this word game.

After reconfirming Joe's permission to record our conversation for accuracy, I hit the "record" button on my audio software program.

Then I began this interview where I've never started any interview before–by discussing virtues.

Chapter 5

THE POWER OF VIRTUES

I'd done my homework before arriving. Grayson HR was a firm with a financial track record that would knock the socks off almost any other firm in the world. Wouldn't most executives want to first focus on revenues, profit, EBITDA, market share growth, or any number of other financial data? Gee, even starting in innovation, R&D, strategy, brand, or customer service made more sense.

But no...although my cynical reporter's instincts suggested challenging Joe, I decided to explore the "virtues" angle and see how it played out. I could always redirect later.

"Joe, it's interesting to me that you pin the success of Grayson HR first and foremost on virtues. That seems like an unexpected place to start. Can you tell me what you mean by virtues?"

Noting Joe's slight but eager nod, I could tell this resonated with him. His eyes alight with enthusiasm, he began telling me his story.

"When I formed Grayson HR, I walked away from corporate America with a distinct bad taste in my mouth. After years of climbing the traditional corporate ladder, and watching helplessly as my ladder was moved, broken, or even removed without notice, I decided it was time to start building the kind of firm I had only dreamed of. This company would be more than just about profits, although profit is something any private firm must attain or you close your doors.

"The men and woman I had worked with were, for the most part, decent, hard working people. As in any firm, some were good, and some were not so good. But what became clear to me as I moved from company to company was this: the higher a person climbed in the firm, the more prone they were to doing stupid things.

"One day, after a particularly tough day, I sat down with one blank notepad in front of me. At the top of the page I wrote, 'Stupid Things I've Seen Leaders Do.' I began listing things like profit at all costs, delaying vendor payments, across-the-board pay cuts, mass firings, not doing what they said they would do, not standing up for what they believed in or said, flying off the handle, not following through on commitments, unwillingness to make the tough decisions, losing focus on their vision, etc.

"After I'd filled a couple of pages, I turned to another page and wrote on the top of it, 'What Leaders Need to Be.' I began brainstorming characteristics of leaders who would not succumb to the stupid things on the first list.

"At the beginning, this was a messy list. Dozens of characteristics popped into my mind. Within twenty minutes, I had completely filled the front of the paper with two columns of words that would be characteristics of great leaders. Words like 'visionary,' 'approachable,' 'takes care of their people,' 'authentic,' 'mentor,' and 'unafraid to do the right thing' came to mind.

"The list was, to say the least, overwhelming. I vividly remember saying to myself, 'There is no way I can become or even remember most of these.' But rather than getting frustrated and stopping, I asked myself a couple of questions.

"First, do any of these words naturally fit together? Is there a natural alignment of these concepts that lend themselves to a list that's easier to remember and implement?"

Joe pulled a notepad in front of him, drew a line down the center of the page, and continued. "I quickly began connecting words that naturally connected, or flowed together, crisscrossing the page from top to bottom with an intricate spider web of connections." With quick, sharp lines, the page in front of Joe took shape as an illustration of this process.

"The second question I asked was, 'Is there a logical heading for these connections, a single word that summarizes the essence of these various concepts? What I quickly found was that they naturally aligned within four major groups. Looking carefully at the groups of words under each title, and then reflecting on the power of their shared connections, I realized these words didn't just tumble together by coincidence. These four areas were actually virtues."

"What do you mean by virtues?" I asked.

Joe leaned forward, speaking slowly and quietly for emphasis.

"A virtue is a special moral quality of excellence. It reflects something deep within people based on their own knowledge of right and wrong. It's a long-held, high-level principle of life lived out within their daily activities. It's their guiding compass, something far more than just laws and rules and regulations and policy manuals."

I bit. I wanted to know more. "So what are the four virtues you came up with?"

Joe wrote down four words. "In their proper order, from first to last, the four virtues are character, competence, courage, and commitment."

With my finely-tuned journalist's powers of observation, I immediately noted, "So, they all start with the letter 'C'."

Joe laughed and nodded. "Right you are, Tony! I know to some it sounds hokey, but that alliteration also makes the words easily memorable. I'm hoping that during your time here today, as you get to know our family, you'll see why they fit together the way they do as well as the critical components of each virtue."

"So there is more to these virtues than just a catchy feel-good list?" I asked with more than a slight hint of sarcasm. Joe seemed like he could take a little teasing.

"Absolutely!" Joe said, pushing his list aside. "Although the list is simple, it's not simplistic. And frankly, I appreciate your initial skepticism."

"Really?" I was actually somewhat amazed he picked up on it. By this point in an interview, most people were so sold on their own story they missed any hint of sarcasm completely.

"Yes, I do. I expect you'll capitalize on that initial skepticism—it's what I think makes you a great reporter. I expect you to ask the tough questions we all need to ask ourselves here. You'll actually help us become better by making us articulate why and how we do what we do. And since you've already promised a totally candid, honest and accurate article, I trust you will indeed follow through."

Well, THAT was unexpected. This guy was good. Not manipulative, but effectively framing the conversation and the outcome within the boundaries he desired. But I reminded myself to withhold final judgment until all the facts were uncovered. This was, remember, the founder. He'd been polishing this speech for years. Surely the real story was somewhere else.

"Okay, Joe, since you say these four virtues are the core to your success, let's dive into the first one. What do you mean by ch...."

Unexpectedly Joe raised his right hand, palm facing me, politely but firmly interrupting me to say, "Hold on now, Tony. You know as well as I do that I can say anything I want to as the founder of Grayson HR, hoping you'll believe me and not question it. But I think your story will be far more authentic if you hear directly from the people working here. I'd like you to build your story on their stories, not mine."

I'd seen this technique before: Joe was going to hand me off to some people he'd pre-positioned to make sure I heard only the good stuff. I got it now.

Then Joe threw me a hanging curve. "I'd like you to roam around the building and talk to anyone you like."

I frowned slightly. "Are you telling me I can talk to anyone I want to about these four virtues and how they drive the success of your business?"

Joe didn't flinch. "Yes."

I squinted thoughtfully at him, wondering, was he for real? Was this a joke? Talk to anyone I chose?

Joe reached onto his desk for a file folder. "I asked Francis to prepare an complete employee list with everyone's name, title, department, and length of time here. Here's a copy. Also attached is a layout of the building. In last week's 'All Team Meeting,' I told everyone that you might ask them some questions for the article, and asked them to answer honestly."

He continued, "Feel free to roam around and talk to whomever you believe will give you the most honest insights on each virtue. All I ask is that you allow some time with me at the end of your visit for an exit discussion. Fair enough?"

I nodded, still mulling over this unusual tactic. Was there a catch? Clicking off the microphone, I quickly slid my computer and notebook back into my bag.

"One last thing," Joe said just before we stood up. "As you interview our people, you'll discover that we don't talk about success in the traditional business ways. Rather, we focus more on significance."

Leaving his office, Joe led me on a quick walking tour of the building, introducing me to people we encountered. Our last stop was an employee break room, where he introduced me to a couple of people before excusing himself and leaving me on my own.

Virtues. Family. Significance. Was all this for real? I decided to find out.

Chapter 6

VIRTUE 1: CHARACTER

The break room was an inviting space with a flat screen TV on an end wall, large windows offering views of the beautifully kept grounds, and doors leading out to a small, shady courtyard furnished with bistro tables and chairs. Instead of the typical institutional motivational posters on the walls, I noticed attractively framed photos of scenes around Bowling Green. Stepping closer, I could see labels near each one with the name of the photographer, the photo's date, and its scene or location.

"I see you've spotted our gallery," a friendly young woman commented. She walked over to me with a smile. "These were all taken by Grayson HR folks. We call it 'family photos.' It's kind of fun seeing how we all see our hometown."

"Are you originally from Bowling Green?" I asked, pleased to find a fellow native. She shook her head. "No, but it's home now, so I call it our hometown." She extended a friendly hand. "I'm Sally Metz, by the way. Very nice to meet you." She indicated a nearby counter set up with a sleek stainless coffee maker system and a tantalizing selection of sugars, creamers, and flavorings. "Would you like a cup of coffee?"

I nodded. "Yes, that sounds great. And wow, your coffee sure smells wonderful."

"It's our special blend roasted by a locally owned coffee shop," Sally explained. She reached for a cup, slipped it into a "Beans on the Green" sleeve, and poured steaming-hot coffee into it. "It's a nice branding opportunity for our customers, but also a special treat for us as well. Sugar? Creamer?"

"No, thank you," I said, accepting the cup. "This is just the way I like my coffee—black and hot."

Sally smiled. "You must be Mr. Sullivan. Welcome to Grayson HR."

"Thank you very much, and please call me Tony. I just met with Joe, and he invited me to talk to anyone here about what makes this place so special."

"Doesn't surprise me," Sally commented. "Joe really sets a fantastic tone around here. Never seen this at any other company."

My ears perked up.

"Do you have time for a few questions, Sally?"

"Sure!" Sally gestured toward the door. "Let's just step into my office down the hall."

As we entered Sally's cheerful, comfortably furnished office, I immediately got a sense of her personality. In place of typical commercial office furniture, she had a beautifully finished antique writing desk, a pair of overstuffed club chairs, and a large cedar armoire in the corner. A soft wool area rug warmed the floor and a colorful watercolor scene of historic Smiths Grove hung on the wall.

Settling into one of the comfortable chairs, Sally pulled a small table forward for my laptop and indicated a nearby electrical outlet in case I needed it. She forwarded her phone calls while I set up my trusty laptop and pulled out my notebook.

Glancing at the employee roster Joe had given me, I saw Sally was the director of worker's compensation, a critically important role in protecting Grayson HR from catastrophic losses due to employees' injuries and lengthy recovery. No doubt this made her a busy person, and I resolved to work quickly.

"As you probably know, Sally, Lens Shift is featuring Grayson HR as their "Spotlight" company this year. I'm here to explore what makes this place so good. What do you think that is?"

"Character," Sally said without a moment's hesitation.

"Character?" I asked, glancing back through my notes. "Joe said that was the first of his four virtues."

Sally nodded. "Tony, everything about Joe Grayson and this company, what we do, how we operate, even how we treat each another and our customers…everything here begins with character."

I was curious. "So how would you define character?"

"Character is the depth of your moral convictions," Sally replied thoughtfully. "It's the ability to distinguish between what's right and what's wrong."

"Moral convictions? You mean ethics?"

"No, Tony, that's not what it means at all," Sally said with a smile. "One of the first lessons we learn during Grayson HR's new employee orientation is the difference between ethics and character. Ethics asks, 'Is it fair and legal?' Character asks, 'Is it just and moral?' You see, character takes us to a higher level of insight and accountability than just ethics."

I made a couple of notes. "Give me an example of how that works here."

"OK, here's a recent example. One of our PEO clients perpetually pushes us to misclassify their employees so they can get a lower workers' compensation rate. They want us to misclassify some part-time heavy equipment field workers as full-time office workers. They know, and we know, this is wrong, both legally and morally. While other PEO's may do this to keep a client, this customer knows Grayson HR won't."

"So you don't do what your client asks you to do?" I squinted at Sally. "What about the old adage 'The customer's always right?'"

"Not when it compromises one of our core virtues."

"Has this stance cost you any business?"

"Absolutely, more than I care to tell you. But I'll tell you something, Tony," Sally said emphatically. "I'd much rather be in a small company that maintains good character than in a large firm with none. We may lose this account or that account, and we have at times. But even when we do, it means everything to be able to look in the mirror and know we did the right thing. No amount of profit can replace lost principles."

Her sincerity was commendable, but my job was to drill down and uncover the rock bottom truth.

"That's an interesting example, Sally, but is this really how Joe sees it, or is all this character talk just for show?"

"No, it's not for show," Sally said. "Joe likens character to your moral mirror, a reflection of who you are deep down inside. Character, then, is based upon something far deeper than an outside law or regulation. It's who you are on the inside. I've heard it described as who you are in the dark, when nobody can see you."

"So why do you think character is the first of your corporate virtues?"

Sally leaned forward. "Because everything we do, say, believe, and fight for is a direct reflection of our character. This is true in every aspect of our lives, personally, socially, spiritually, and professionally."

I couldn't resist. "So Grayson HR is morally superior to all the other HR outsourcing companies in America. Is that what you're telling me?"

"No, not at all." Sally smiled, with no hint of defensiveness. "It's just that we have clearly defined the moral standards by which we operate, and we hold everyone accountable to them."

As a journalist, I 'd developed a well-rehearsed poker face, but I could tell that Sally immediately picked up on my skepticism.

"I was just as confused when I first heard this" she said. "Joe describes it this way. He likens character to a swimming pool. At one end is the shallow end with a set of steps that slowly takes you into waist-deep water. At the other end is the deep end, where the water is way over your head."

"Some people only wade into the shallow end of the character pool. They'll say things like, 'We treat our people right,' but then at the first hint of hard times, they lay off employees in a New York minute. Others have deep-seated convictions and will do everything possible to keep their employees on board or assist them in finding other employment."

Sally continued, "Lip service, Tony. I know you've seen it. Too many companies today pay lip service to their values. But when the going gets tough, they back down and try to do only what's fair and legal, the shallow end, rather than what is just and moral, the deep end."

"That's a good analogy," I replied. "But it begs the question, 'Whose morals?'"

I think Sally was ready for this question. She smiled and said, "That's exactly what I thought when I first heard it. Let me show you how we teach character at Grayson HR."

She stood and stepped over to a small blank whiteboard hanging on the wall next to her desk where she wrote the following words:

CHARACTER: DEPTH OF CONVICTIONS

-> Wisdom - knowing what is right

-> Integrity - doing what is right

-> Self-discipline - keep doing it

"According to Joe, there are three components of character. The first is wisdom. Wisdom is defined as knowing what's is right. All of us have an internal anchor, our 'moral compass' if you will, that tells us what we believe is right and what we believe is wrong. That anchor is based upon a set of principles, values, teachings, and philosophies, something unique to each person. It's up to us individually to decide on our basis for wisdom."

"So what's Joe's moral compass?"

"The Bible."

Great. One of THOSE companies. I zeroed in quickly.

"But not everyone believes in the Bible, or even thinks it belongs in business."

"That's correct," Sally agreed. "And that's fine. Here's how it works here. Our approach is that it's the leader's primary duty to consciously choose the moral foundation of the organization, to clearly define what is right and what is not right to do. Wisdom, therefore, is knowing what is right, regardless of the situation."

I finished jotting her notes into my notebook. "Give me an example of how this all fits together."

"That's pretty easy, actually," Sally said, resuming her seat across from me. "Let's say that as a leader you know the right thing to do is to pay your suppliers within thirty days of receiving their invoice. We tell them that it's our policy, that we believe that's just the wise, and right, thing to do. They have already provided a service that cost them time, money, payroll, and materials, and we need to pay their bill."

"Now let's say Grayson HR is having a cash flow crunch. For whatever reason, we decide that this month we can't pay them within thirty days and we decide to pay them after forty-five days, or even sixty days, with no explanation to them. Our integrity comes into play, and from their perspective, our character. Some of the companies I've worked with in the past just say, 'Hey, that's business.' At Grayson HR, we see it as much more."

"Finally, our self-discipline determines if we will pay them first even when it's tough. Self-discipline is the final step in determining the depth of our moral convictions. We could occasionally display integrity when it's easy or convenient and doesn't cost us much. The real test of our character is whether we do the right thing even when it hurts."

"So you see," Sally concluded, "wisdom is the first component of character, but is not enough. Your character is revealed not so much by what you believe, but by what you do, and especially by what you do when it costs you something."

I had to admit this made a lot of sense to me. I had seen this played out too many times, both before joining Lens Shift and now in investigating dozens of fallen firms. They lauded magnificently-worded value statements only to be crushed when they got caught not following them. Reminded me of Enron's spectacular fall and their touted four values, one of which was integrity. Even listed them at the bottom of their letterhead. If only they'd met Joe!

But something still nagged at me. "I appreciate your time in explaining your first virtue of character." I told Sally. "And yes, I can see how this would indeed serve as the foundation of everything you do here. But since Joe claims he uses the Bible as his wisdom foundation, I guess that means he only hires fellow Bible believers."

"On no, far from it!" exclaimed Sally. "We in no way exclude anyone from employment consideration if they don't believe the Bible. We simply let everyone who applies to work here know that the fundamental precepts we use as the foundation of our wisdom are biblically based, and that everyone, including Joe, is held accountable for following these wisdom principles in their work. Everyone then has the right to opt in or opt out."

She glanced out the window. "That's why I opted in and accepted their job offer. Moved from over four hundred miles away. I wandered around here during my interviews, talked to lots of folks, kind of like you're doing today, and determined they all meant it. And yes, I was particularly drawn to this first virtue. I decided to bet my career on it, and so far, I'm thrilled with my choice."

Sally's conviction to this virtue of character was nothing short of amazing, I thought. She bought into it, believed it, saw it at work all around her. Anyone who met her could sense it.

I decided to move to virtue #2–competence.

"If it's okay with you, Sally, can we move on to the next virtue–competence?"

"Nope," she said firmly but politely. "Don't want to do that."

"Why not? You don't believe in it?"

"Oh no, it's not that. It's just that if I were you, I'd want more than just one or two opinions. Why don't you speak to our Director of People, Rebecca Godfrey, on competence? She heads up most of our internal and external training and development and has a unique perspective on how this virtue is taught and lived within Grayson HR."

I agreed immediately, and once again packed up my computer and notebook. Thanking Sally for her time and input, I noted her wide, contagious smile and firm handshake. Far from being corporate zombiespeak, her emphatic "My pleasure!" was immediate and sincere.

Chapter 7

VIRTUE 2: COMPETENCE

Rebecca's office was close to the main entrance, as most human resource offices tend to be. I imagined that was because the HR department was usually the first place people visited when they joined a firm and the last place they visited when they left, whether voluntarily or involuntarily.

A friendly, polished woman with dark hair and an easy smile, Rebecca seemed accustomed to putting people at ease in her office. She invited me to sit at a small conference table, offered me refreshments, and waited while I quickly set up my computer and pulled out my notebook. As we both settled in for the interview, Rebecca surprised me by asking, "So tell me, Tony, what are your first three impressions of Grayson HR?"

I reminded myself that I was in the presence of another professional interviewer, a person comfortable with being in charge of a conversation.

"Well, Rebecca, my first three impressions would be that Grayson HR is professional, focused, and friendly. Is that what you wanted to hear?"

With a smile, Rebecca quickly replied, "Oh no, Tony. Every person, every employee, has character flaws. We're far from perfect, so I was asking for a candid assessment through the eyes of an unbiased observer. You can't get that every day, can you?"

"No, I suppose not, not even in the best firms," I admitted. "The way we write the 'Spotlight' features, you'd think everyone at the company walked on water, but even the best of the best have flaws."

I remembered conducting an in-depth case study of Southwest Airlines, before they became a daily "best practice" company. After giving over-the-top glowing praise for all the progressive ways, the then-VP of Human Resources looked at me sternly and said, "Tony, all you've done is tell me how great this is and how wonderful that is. I've been at Southwest Airlines for over 10 years and I constantly see the politics, budget, and talent challenges. Tell me—are we really that good?" I reassured here they were.

"Sally gave me a wonderful overview of the first virtue at Grayson HR: character," I explained. "She suggested you might be the best person to teach me about your second virtue— competence."

Nodding thoughtfully, Rebecca replied, "Let me begin with an overview, then give you some specific examples." I could see the trainer coming out in her–always let the audience know where you are going. Same is true with a business journalist, I mused.

"As you know, character around here means the depth of your moral convictions," Rebecca said. "Everything starts there. Competence, then, is the strength of your skills. We teach that even for those with powerful convictions, without competence, the convictions go nowhere.

"Now I'm sure you're already seeing, Tony, that we start at a completely different place than most companies. They typically start with recruiting, hiring, and promoting people based on their skills and abilities. We absolutely believe skills are critical, but a highly skilled person without the right convictions can be dangerous."

I must admit, after all my years in business, I had not heard this said before as succinctly or as clearly. Very rational. Very practical. Very well articulated.

"OK, Rebecca, for the sake of time I'll stipulate that character trumps competence for now, but the bigger question is, how do you teach competence? What does competence look like at Grayson HR?"

"Well, Tony, let me share a little secret of our culture," Rebecca replied. "One of Joe's most popular sayings around here is, 'Simple is not simplistic, so let's keep things simple.' We all know that business is very complex, but our solutions and responses don't need to be. Too many companies severely overcomplicate their approach to team competencies, with all kinds of models, lists, procedures, measures, and unnecessary expense.

"So we constantly strive to take the complexity out of skill, knowledge, and attitude development. Although we offer dozens of learning opportunities to our people, from in-house workshops, cross-training, webinars, college tuition reimbursement, and many more, we teach all levels of competencies within a simple yet powerful three-part competency model."

With that, she retrieved a tablet from her desk, opened an application, and used a stylus to draw three overlapping circles with the word 'Competence' above the circles. Inside the first circle, she wrote the word, 'Envision.'

"Envision answers the fundamental question, 'What's next?' This is where we focus on how to think clearly, strategize, assess the environment surrounding the decision, and determine what should be the next move. Envisioning for us is not some mystical, esoteric dream—it's applying sharp analytics to what the next steps must be in order to meet our goals."

Rebecca glanced at me to make sure I was following. "For Joe and all of us on the executive team, envisioning includes long-range strategic planning, alliances, competitor analysis, and all the traditional senior level strategic concerns."

Inside the next circle, Rebecca wrote the word 'Engage.'

"While envisioning is all about the 'what,' engaging is all about the 'who.' Engaging answers the question of who needs to be involved in what's next, whether inside or outside the firm. It also answers when they need to be involved. For us, being involved is all about the 'who,' that is, the people."

Inside the last circle, Rebecca wrote 'Execute.'

"For Grayson HR, execution is all about the how and the when—in other words, the results. Here is where we create the launch plan, from timing, materials, and all, to how we measure progress, who inspects and redirects progress, and how we celebrate reaching the goals."

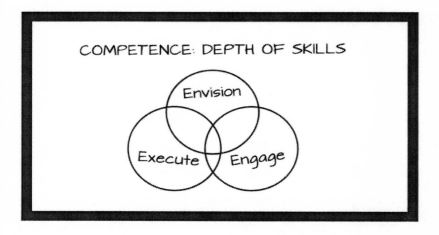

As I listened carefully and wrote quickly, I concluded that this E3 model was nothing really revolutionary. Any successful company integrated these concepts within their operations, some to a greater degree than others.

"So you're telling me, Rebecca, that your E3 competence model for your executive team is one of your great keys to success?"

"No, not at all," she said calmly. "The real power of our approach to competencies, Tony, is that we take this same E3 model into all levels of the organization. It's not just for the senior leadership. It's the same model all front-line leaders use as well. We also do the same thing with engagement and execution skills for all levels. What this does is make sure that everyone is playing out of the same playbook, to coin a football analogy. I prefer to say we're all chefs cooking from the same recipe!"

I'm sure my skepticism showed. Had Grayson HR fallen into the all-too-common trap of corporate lingo and consultant talk?

Perhaps she sensed my disillusionment with this approach. I told you she was a professional interviewer! At any rate, Rebecca asked, "Would you like to see how this works in person?"

"Absolutely," I responded, anxious to get out of the office and see the concepts in action.

She clicked on another app on her tablet, navigated to a calendar feature, and said, "It looks like Safety is conducting an E3 session right now. Let's go take a peek."

Chapter 8

From Success to Significance

David Justin was midway through his E3 session with his staff, two business development consultants, an underwriter, and Sally from worker's compensation. He paused for a moment, made introductions and welcomed me to the meeting, and dove back into the discussion. On the white board on the front wall of the room, I could see the first E for Envision had four key goals. From that circle, they were now discussing the second E–Engage.

In my experience, the designated leader and/or the highest-ranking participant dominate most meetings in business. Most other attendees simply nod in agreement and act like they are interested. Not this team.

Although Dave had called the meeting and could have easily dominated, he kept the conversation focused, fast, flexible, and fun. He kept it moving, on target, allowing for just the right amount of creativity and adjustments, and upbeat.

As the meeting concluded, Dave dismissed everyone and came over to shake my hand.

"Thank you for joining us," he said warmly. "Dave Justin, Director of Workplace Safety. I must say your presence helped me stay a little better on target than normal, although I should probably not admit that to you, Rebecca." The two exchanged grins.

Dave was one of the more senior members of the Grayson HR team, at least of those I'd met so far. I guessed he was about five years older than me, probably in his mid 50's. Since we were close in age, I felt comfortable asking him a couple of probing questions.

"May I ask you, Dave, how long you've been with Grayson HR?"

"Two years."

I was surprised, and it showed.

"I expected you'd been here longer."

He pointed to his silver hair with a laugh. "What, from the amount of gray up here? Tony, I earned every one these after surviving thirty-plus years with other companies that didn't get it."

"Didn't get what?"

"That business isn't all about success—it's about significance."

I shook my head. "Dave, come on. We've both been around a while. Please don't try to convince me that Grayson HR has some magic formula where success doesn't matter. Every firm needs to be successful. Significant? Not so sure."

His smile now gone, Dave paused to choose his words carefully. "With all due respect, Tony, what you've just said is exactly where most companies miss it. They think everything they do is only about the profit, prestige, and power that come with traditional business. Here, we take everything we do to a higher level, including our team meetings."

"Profit, prestige, and power." I'd retrieved my notebook and was writing furiously in my own shorthand. "Dave, that sounds like a winning combination to me. It takes profit to keep the business going, prestige to attract and retain the best people and customers, and power to influence markets and leverage growth."

Dave saw my response coming.

"Tony, I could take issue with your analysis, but let me say this. The skills you saw me demonstrate in this team meeting could be used for good or bad. Is profit in and of itself bad? Of course not. Is prestige? No. Is power? Not necessarily. What I take issue with, though, and what separates us from 98% of other firms, is that we base everything we do on our corporate character. We don't start with competence."

Dave's gaze intensified.

"Grayson HR is dedicated to moving through success to significance. We refuse to stay stuck on profit, prestige, or power. In fact, we use an entirely different set of words to describe what we focus on. Would you like to know them?"

"Of course!" I was hooked.

"We go from a traditional business focus of profit, prestige, and power to a higher level where we focus our efforts on purpose, principles, and people. I'm sure to an outsider this all sounds a bit hokey. It did to me when I first visited here two years ago, too. I was as cynical as the day was long, having worked for companies that had no purpose outside of maximizing shareholder value, no principles outside of making more money, and people were only there to do their work and shut up."

Dave was playing right into my own background. That's exactly what I had experienced and wanted to escape. He continued.

"Let me tell you, Tony, the one thing it takes to move from a focus of success to significance. It doesn't necessarily take a personal or spiritual conversion. It only takes courage."

I had to admit Dave had a point. It only took a nanosecond to think back on all the lousy corporate cultures and pitiful excuses for leaders I once toiled beneath. Not one of them had one ounce of courage to do the right thing, only the most profitable thing.

After a short silence, Rebecca, who had remained in the room, spoke up. "Tony, I think this is a good segue into you learning about our third virtue, courage."

I glanced at my watch. It was close to noon. I knew I needed to eat something soon or I would get a monster headache.

"I agree. How about I jump out for some lunch and be back here at, say, 1:30?"

"We'd be glad to take you to lunch," both Dave and Rebecca offered.

I politely declined. "If it's all right, I'd like to take some time to study my notes and reflect on what I've seen and heard so far. It's like my wife says, if I don't write it down, I'll forget it."

Dave and Rebecca agreed immediately. I asked for a lunch recommendation, and they suggested Beans on the Green, a local eatery nearby. From his notebook, Dave extracted a card and handed it to me.

"If you'll present them with this card, you'll get twenty percent off whatever you order there."

"What's good on the menu?"

"I try to have something different each time I'm there," Dave admitted. "So far they've hit a home run every time."

Chapter 9

BEANS ON THE GREEN

My GPS had no trouble directing me to the restaurant a few blocks away. Fortunate enough to snag a parking spot near the entrance, I noted the clever preservation of old tiles in the sidewalk outside the entrance. The word "Hungry?" had been attracting diners for generations, I imagined.

Inside, I found myself in a bright, airy café furnished with eclectic tables and chairs. Colorful posters, vintage ads, and antique kitchen tools brightened the walls. Ceiling fans suspended from a timeworn tin ceiling traced lazy circles overhead, stirring the air and sending the heavenly fragrance of freshly baked bread and roasted coffee beans past the noses of patrons patiently waiting their turn at the counter.

There was a happy hubbub of people working behind the counter, and I stepped into line and studied the menu chalkboards. Clever names and descriptions abounded, and it took me a few minutes to narrow down my selection—a spinach salad with chicken and fresh fruit, and a drink called "Autumn Sunset"—their signature house blend coffee made with vanilla and hazelnut syrup and topped with cinnamon whipped cream. I placed my order, paid, picked up my order number, and turned to scope out the café.

Most of the tables and booths were filled, but I snagged a seat at the busy counter. The lunch break was just what I needed—great food, the hustle and flow of the restaurant all around me, and time to organize my thoughts before diving back into the article.

A friendly woman wearing a bright yellow Beans on the Green apron briskly checked the status of a fresh pot of coffee, wiped down the counter, and refilled the napkin dispenser near me. I noticed that even when she was standing still for a minute or two, her eyes were on the move, constantly assessing who might need what in the busy eatery. People frequently greeted her as they entered and left, and she exuded quiet, friendly efficiency.

"Busy day for you today?" I asked. She glanced at me with a smile.

"About normal for this time of day," she said. She stepped into the kitchen area.

Moments later, she returned with my lunch, placed it in front of me and asked, "Would you like a glass of water, or some extra napkins?"

"No, no, I'm fine, but thanks for asking." I took a chance. "Are you the manager or the owner here?"

"Mary Frasier." She smiled at someone who called out to her on their way out the door. "Thanks, Dan!" Her gaze returned to me. "Yes, I'm the owner."

"Let me ask you a question, if you have just a minute?"

"Sure." She slid a piece of the most delicious looking pie I'd ever seen out of a nearby case and handed it to a server. "No ice cream on that one, Belle."

I pulled a notebook and pen from my jacket pocket and opened it quickly, although my mind was still on that pie.

"I'm Tony Sullivan with Lens Shift magazine, and I'm here to learn about Grayson HR. I understand you provide them with coffee for their offices?"

"Yes…" Mary squinted at me thoughtfully. "If you're looking to get me to spill the beans, so to speak, on Grayson, you're probably asking the wrong person. But I'm happy to talk with you about our relationship with Grayson HR and what it allows us to do."

"What it allows you to do?" Mary caught me off guard.

"We do provide them with coffee and supplies for their employees, and we help with catering sometimes when they need that. Joe Grayson is a great guy. He approached us a few years ago when they were setting up shop. Turns out he had heard about something we were doing and he wanted to know how he could help."

"Joe wanted to help you?" I was confused.

"Yes. Apparently he'd heard about something we've done for years, working with friends of ours who are missionaries in South America. These friends work with coffee bean growers there, making contacts for them in the states so they can sell their beans for more money than the big coffee companies pay. By helping our friends, we're also supporting South American farmers and maybe giving them a chance to hear some really good news that will change their lives forever."

Mary turned to answer a question from a young server waiting near her elbow. I knew that was about all the time she could spare during a busy lunch hour, and I thanked her for her time and her story.

"Of course. Joe Grayson is a good friend. Looking forward to reading your article." She reached beneath the counter and pulled out a plate holding a slice of pie, berries tumbling like jewels from beneath a flaky golden crust. She set a fork near my hand. "That's our signature cherry berry pie—and this one's on the house."

Wondering if I should message Bart that the story needed to take a culinary turn, I made short work of my salad and the pie. The coffee was indeed good, some of the best I'd had in a while.

I left a larger than normal tip with my check. Great service and great food was worth it.

Chapter 10

VIRTUE 3: COURAGE

Since Joe gave me full approval to meet with anyone I chose, and since everyone at Grayson HR already knew I was on site, I re-entered the building through a side door near what appeared to be a delivery entrance with a roll-up door.

Inside this part of the building, the walls were decorated with pictures, paintings, and posters celebrating Grayson HR's people and history. It strongly reminded me of the Southwest Airlines headquarters buildings at Love Field in Dallas. In both places, people could learn the history of the firms simply by wandering up and down the hallways, enjoying the vibrant collages of company celebrations, awards, and even photos of employees' new babies.

One poster really caught my attention. It was a promotion for a "Cancer Freedom Day: An Alternative Approach." As I scanned the announcement of special workshops, an organic food lunch, and giveaways, I heard someone directly behind me say, "A lot of people stop and read that one."

Billy Linnville reached out his hand and introduced himself. I commented on how unusual it was that Grayson HR would bring in special speakers and dedicate an entire day to such a timely and controversial topic.

"Not surprising at all, really," Billy shrugged. "It's pretty common around here. You've probably heard about how important wisdom is around here, so we actively look for anything that does not directly oppose the Bible and opens up opportunities for everyone that's interested to participate."

He paused, and then quickly added, "Oh, I guess you've heard that Joe uses the Bible for the foundation of his company."

"Yes, I've learned that," I said. "It intrigues me as to why, but I'll take that up with Joe a little later."

I again glanced at the poster, and realized the main speaker for "Cancer Freedom Day" was none other than Billy Linnville!

"So this is something you know about?"

Billy nodded.

"I'm a cancer survivor."

"Congratulations. You must have quite a story."

"Indeed. In fact, I have to tell you that the approach we take here at Grayson helped me face and overcome cancer."

He pointed to a nearby doorway. "My office is just around the corner—would you like to know why I say that?"

There was no questioning Billy's loyalty. A University of Florida Gators flag hung prominently from the back wall and a large Al E. Gator plush animal perched on his credenza, a gift from his daughter who attended the University of Florida.

"I've been a member of the Grayson HR family for twelve years," Billy began. "I've worked my way up from underwriting and sales and now am the Director of Benefits. I oversee and advise all our clients on how to maximize their employee benefits."

"During my standard annual check up eight years ago, my blood work indicated an abnormally high level of white blood cells. After some X-rays, we learned I had an enlarged spleen. My first decision was whether to have surgery, and if so, when. Since surgery was inevitable, my wife and I decided to have it then. And we are forever glad I did.

"My spleen was so enlarged with cancer cells that it had doubled over; when removed, it was one and a half times larger than the x-rays showed. Had we not gone in immediately, I dread to think what could have happened.

"The cancer prognosis was profound, to say the least. The cancerous cells were floating around in my body. Although we didn't have to do anything immediately, we knew we needed to make a decision on how to approach the future. I had to look deep within myself to clarify my core convictions on how to approach this disease.

"My heart and soul told me that I should take a natural and holistic approach, not the traditional medical radiation and chemo approach. Please don't misunderstand me. I have nothing at all against any traditional medical treatment or the miracles of modern medicine. Quite the opposite. I just knew, down deep, that I needed to go a different route than the prevailing current wisdom.

"But I had no knowledge or competence in a natural, holistic approach to cancer treatment. That's when I decided to read and learn all I could. I envisioned the result (cancer free), got engaged with high quality information sources and experts, then developed and began executing my plan.

"Did it take courage to take make the decision and take the first step? Yes indeed. Some say I was a fool. Some even today contend I am. But as my knowledge grew and I experienced success, so did my confidence. And as my confidence in what I was doing grew, my composure grew to help me weather the ups and downs, the good days and bad ones. I was better able to remain rather calm and under control; not totally stress free, mind you. But as my confidence grew, so did my composure to face whatever was ahead, even when I didn't know what that might be.

"Today I've been cancer free for over seven years. I have gained the confidence to share my story, my path, and my knowledge with others in the 'Cancer Free Day' Workshop. You see, it did take courage to take the first step, but that courage grew rapidly as I continued acting on my character convictions and the competence in the new learning."

Even though I might not have completely agreed with Billy's approach to medicine, I had to admit it was impressive how he'd based his decisions on first his character and convictions, and gained the competence he needed to address the issue.

It made perfect sense to me, then, how his courage grew as a consequence of his confidence, composure and boldness.

Billy continued, "Think about it, Tony. It takes courage to make many of the decisions we make every day. Some take just a little courage, like buying office supplies from a new constituent, and others take far more courage, like terminating a long-term employee for dishonesty. In either case, those decisions must be based first upon your wisdom, integrity, and self-discipline, and then on how you envision the situation, engage those necessary, and develop your plan to execute the decision. Over time, your confidence will grow as well your composure, which automatically leads to being bolder in your decisions and ultimately affects the quality of the outcome.

"And that's the way we teach courage. We define courage as the willingness to act upon your convictions. But you should never act on them without competence. Your competence grows confidence that leads to composure that ultimately moves you toward boldness."

This time I wrote down the key concepts on my notepad.

COURAGE: ACT ON CONVICTIONS

-> Confidence

-> Composure

-> Boldness

"That's impressive indeed, Billy. But it seems to me that being bold enough to tell a colleague he is misclassifying employees or close to breaking the law must be tough."

Billy nodded.

"Tony, this is something we fight every single day. It would be easy to look the other way or make exceptions, but you know as well as I do that so often that one exception slowly creeps into the corporate culture and becomes the way we do things, because, hey, the customer is the customer and we need the income."

I remembered many times in previous jobs and particularly in my investigative reporting seeing well-meaning business professionals take that first small step on the slippery slope of shifting ethics that soon became a tsunami of epic ethical failures.

Tucking my notepad in my pocket, I thanked Billy for his time, his story, and his candor. He encouraged me to follow up if I needed any additional information.

Leaving his office, I walked down the hall, thinking things over. No question about it, the Grayson HR approach was logical, sensible, and seemed to apply to staff members in their business and personal lives.

Yet to me, the most fascinating part so far was seeing Grayson HR's business leadership and personal leadership model. So far I'd seen people employ this approach in both their work and their personal lives. That was rare indeed for any traditional leadership model.

But I had to admit it only made sense that a non-traditional company like Grayson HR would be based on a non-traditional leadership model.

Chapter 11

VIRTUE 4: COMMITMENT

Rounding a corner, I found myself in a big, brightly lit room. A large work table on wheels dominated the center of the room. An energetic woman was working alongside two young people that looked like they might be interns–my reporter's sharp eye spotted their name tags and "intern" title right away. As I paused, the woman glanced up and greeted me with a wide smile.

"I wondered if you might make your way back here!" she exclaimed. As I held out my hand to introduce myself, she grabbed it firmly and said, "I know who you are, of course. I'm Elaine Tabor, but everyone calls me Laney. Pleasure to meet you."

"Thank you, Laney. The feeling is mutual."

"Come on in! This is our BDC resource center," Laney said. I noted the custom-built birch cubbies holding everything from pens and notepads to corporate 'swag' for various events. Underneath the worktable were stools that could be rolled away when they weren't needed for seating. Checklists on the walls facilitating packet content consistency were interspersed with vintage railroad and Corvette advertising posters. On the end wall, I admired a replica neon sign from the Capitol Theater downtown. "What a great workspace!" I said. Laney nodded.

"This is where we put together the Grayson HR experience," she told me. "We try to do more than our clients and constituents expect, beginning with their very first impression of our company. We assemble information packets here, and conference materials, and even gift baskets for our family members and for guests coming in from out of town." I noted the stash of Grayson HR water bottles, napkins with corporate logos, and a host of other 'branding opportunities.'

Laney pulled out a stool and invited me to take a seat. She sat opposite me, keeping an eye on the interns still assembling packets.

"Laney, what is your role here?" I asked, quickly retrieving my computer.

"I'm one of Grayson HR's Business Development Consultants, or BDC's as we call them. A BDC is a mix of sales, marketing, and customer development, with a large emphasis on customer development."

"What do you mean by customer development?"

"After we have targeted the top firms in our PoD's to approach..."

"A PoD?" I interjected.

"Sorry. A PoD is what we call our 'Point of Dominance.' It defines what piece of what market we want to own."

"That sounds a little aggressive for a firm based on the Bible," I noted. "Can you give me an example?"

"Well, we simply want to be seen as #1 in our PoD's. That's all. For example, one of our PoD's is Assisted Living Facilities. Our platforms of payroll, workman's compensation, safety, and benefits align perfectly with the needs of these facilities. So within the entire range of assisted living facilities, our PoD is focusing on companies with five or more locations within 500 miles of one another."

I nodded. "That's interesting. I can see how the sales, marketing, and customer development all overlap. I appreciate the description, and it sounds like you're the perfect person to help me understand Grayson HR's fourth C—commitment."

Laney's whole countenance lit up while her eyes still "minded the store," where the interns were continuing to pull items from cubbies and assemble packets.

"Well, Tony, commitment at Grayson HR means being dedicated to a long-term course of action. Frankly, this is the primary reason most of us stay here and stay productive."

"Explain to me how this works." I hit the 'record' button.

"Commitment is where the impact really occurs," Laney said.

I bit. "Impact?"

"Yes, impact," Laney said. "Around here, when somebody makes a commitment, they better mean it, because they're expected to stay true to their word. Whether it's as simple as a commitment from one family member to another to help on a special project or as potentially complex as maintaining a dynamic, positive long-term commitment to a customer, at Grayson HR we're all expected to honor our commitments. Let me tell you about one of my customers. We'll call them ABC Assisted Living, although that's not their real name."

"When I signed on ABC over six years ago, they were profitable, growing, and a vibrant fan of our company. We saved them tens of thousands of dollars in payroll and benefits costs. They were thriving and growing. Then, without warning, the bottom fell out. Through no fault of their own, their parent company decided to liquidate and quickly began selling all their subsidiaries. ABC was on the sales block."

"After a few venture capital firms toyed with buying them, the ABC management team decided to attempt a leveraged buyout. With so much capital and cash flow now invested in legal fees and fights, ABC started falling behind in their payments to us. They needed us more than ever; they just couldn't afford us."

"Realizing they'd been a long-term customer, and knowing that if they were successful in their buyout, they would remain so for years to come, we committed to do everything we could to help them succeed. Without being asked, we approached them with a revised contract and developed a special one-year tiered repayment plan, something we've not done before or since. We made all our resources and team members available to help them get through the negotiations. In particular, we sent teams of human resource and payroll experts to their sites to help train and calm their employees during this stressful time."

Laney sighed as she recounted the challenges of this decision. "The additional time and expenses we incurred during this was tough on us, too. Our cash flow took quite a hit for several months. We had to delay some equipment upgrades we needed, and stay lean in staffing a little while longer. This commitment meant longer hours and an increased workload for many of us. But together we made the commitment to do it and make it work."

"After a long, tough process, their management was successful in buying the firm. After the papers were signed, their very first order of business was to reinstate our original contract and extend it another three years."

"Most other PEO's would have dropped ABC faster than a hot potato. But our commitment was so obvious and profound, we knew ABC would be a customer for life and continue to be one of our most vocal allies within their industry. And that's worth more than any marketing or sales campaign we could ever dream up."

Laney's pride in how Grayson HR handled this tough situation was obvious.

"Well, that's a great illustration, but can you explain to me more specifically how you make commitment such an important part of your culture here?" I asked. Laney thought a moment, and then nodded.

"As I told you earlier, we see commitment as the dedication to a long-term course of action. We believe there are three critical components of Commitment: Purpose, Payoff, and Perseverance."

I noted them on my pad.

```
COMMITMENT: LONG-TERM ACTION

    -> Purpose

    -> Payoff

   -> Perseverance
```

"Tony, think about it this way. When someone makes a commitment to something, say, learning how to play golf, the first thing they determine is the 'why.' Why do I want to play golf? In other words, they're defining their purpose in playing golf. The more compelling the 'why,' the more likely it is they'll stay committed to it."

"Well said," I replied, "but is purpose enough for true commitment?"

"No it's not," Laney agreed. "Purpose is the necessary starting point, but you must add the payoff of the purpose. I could say that the purpose for why I'm committed to golf is to learn a new hobby. But without a payoff in mind, it has no teeth, no real holding power; it's just a good idea."

"The payoff for learning how to play golf," she continued, "could be anything from joining my husband and his friends in a recreational activity, releasing some of my innate competitiveness, or a hobby with the added benefit of some light exercise. Purpose without a clear and compelling payoff will not end in a long-term commitment."

"But there's one more piece to the commitment puzzle," Laney said. "With a clear purpose in mind attached to a powerful payoff, we are far more likely to persevere when times get rough. The best example I can give you of this is a marriage."

That hit close to home.

"In order to succeed, each partner needs to agree on the basic purpose of their marriage and focus on the payoff of their commitment, which gives them the energy to persevere through the tough times," Laney explained. I could see this at work in my own marriage, and began seeing how it played out at Grayson HR as well.

"So these virtues you learn and practice at work can reach into your personal life as well," I noted. Laney nodded eagerly.

"That's exactly right, Tony. These are leadership virtues. That means whether we are at work or at home, we can apply them to make our lives have a great impact." Her eyes twinkled with amusement. "Has anyone told you Joe's nickname around here?"

Chuckling, I replied, "No. Are you going to let me in on this great secret?"

"OK," she said. "But don't tell anyone I told you." She leaned in like a true conspirator. "Joe Grayson's nickname around here is…The Impacter!"

"The Impacter?" I mulled it over. "Must say, that is pretty catchy. Probably better than the Compactor, or the Retractor, or…"

"I think he kind of likes it," Laney said. "It pretty well summarizes everything about him. Joe is all about having an impact on everyone he meets. He often goes out of his way to do just that. And being a strong man of faith, that adds an eternal angle on his desire to impact everyone he meets."

"Eternal?" I frowned, a bit puzzled. "That's sure a long time."

"Yes, but in Joe's mind, that's all that really counts. He knows none of us will last for long on this planet. So whatever good we do must be done quickly or it will just fade away. He wants to make sure the good he does counts for eternity."

"Interesting." I glanced over my notes, not exactly sure how to work that angle into my story.

Thanking Laney for her time and her candor, I packed up my laptop and notepad once again and decided to call it a day.

On my way out of the building, I stopped by Francis' desk to ask about meeting with Joe again the next day. Francis quickly pulled up Joe's calendar, found an afternoon time slot and scheduled me for my 'exit interview,' as Joe called it.

Returning to my hotel, I thought about the many people I'd met that day, and how every one of them seemed to have "drunk the 4-C's Kool-Aid." But this Kool-Aid was different.

It was real, not phony.

Lived, not talked.

Visible, not hidden.

I knew I had to find a way to verify whether this place was for real, or if I had just been the passenger on a very, very well executed corporate public relations ride.

Glancing in the mirror, I knew exactly where to find my answers.

Chapter 12

THE BARBER SHOP

Although many of Bowling Green's newer and most modern hotels and restaurants were close to Scottsville Road on the outskirts of town, I picked a different place to hear the non-biased truth about Grayson HR. The best place was in the middle of downtown, the old, beautifully preserved and renovated center of 'old' Bowling Green.

Downtown Bowling Green is typical of many towns throughout Kentucky: a town square with four or more streets converging around a park or courthouse in the center of the square. The town square of Bowling Green is much larger than most similar towns with a wonderful park, beautiful historic fountain, and well-kept sidewalks winding their way among the thick trees and benches scattered throughout the shaded walkways.

All four sides of this large square are fronted with historic brick buildings housing a variety of offices, eclectic shops, and trendy eateries. It's an appealing mix of 20th century storefronts with occasional unexpected architectural touches like vintage signage, tiled sidewalks advertising businesses from years past, and bold paint colors.

I knew what I was looking for. After twice slowly circling the square, I found it. In front of a small building just south of the square on the west side of College Street I saw a simple sign and striped pole advertising Jones Barber Shop. Again, typical of a Kentucky town: a lovely downtown area with a been-here-since-the-Great Depression, locally owned barbershop.

Barbershops and hair salons are among the best places in America to get uncensored, unsolicited, totally candid opinions on all things political, social, and local. You can learn almost as much about a person in their 'hair studio' as you can on the golf course—but that's a story for another time.

Mid-morning was typically a great time to get a haircut since most customers were either retired, self-employed, business owners with flexible schedules, or salesmen telling their boss they were meeting with another hot prospect.

Inside the shop, five barber chairs faced the mirrored south wall with a single chair at the west end of the open room facing the front door. I imagined the lone chair was for the most senior "Jones" in the room. Several empty customer chairs lined the south wall.

Prominently displayed along the walls were the expected Western Kentucky University paraphernalia including a signed, framed picture of Jim McDaniels, one of several All American basketball players from Western, and several pictures of Big Red, the team's award-winning mascot, along with action shots of other sports teams.

I immediately caught the familiar scents of talcum, disinfectant, and...what was that other smell...popcorn? At the southwest corner of the room stood a popcorn machine with its warmer lamp beaming down upon the gallon of popped corn resting in its base. It was a sight and smell reminiscent of ballparks, movie theaters, and now barbershops.

The first time a new face enters a barbershop, most conversation stops and everyone glances toward the door. This shop was no exception. Three customers occupied the three middle seats along the long wall.

The last chair on the right had a small amount of cut hair encircling its base, and its owner had to be the man approaching with the broom in his hand and a determined look on his face. He smiled and asked, "Like a cut?"

As I walked past the caped customers and their glances, I introduced myself to the barber. I noticed on his work station a framed license with "Monty Jones" printed on it.

"Are you the Jones in the shop name?" I asked.

"Well, I've got barbering in my blood," the man replied. He explained that this was his shop but his grandfather had started the business in this building in 1939. Monty was the third generation of Jones to run it.

"You new in town?" Monty asked, settling a cape around me and pinning it against my neck. I spoke loudly enough for all to hear, but not so loudly as to dominate the quiet conversations occurring around the room.

"Actually, I'm a writer for Lens Shift magazine in Chicago, here to do a feature article on Grayson HR."

"Grayson HR, huh?" Monty was already squinting at my hair, sizing it up. "Good company. Just need a trim today?"

I nodded. "Yeah, a trim would be great. Thanks."

"Some of the Grayson HR guys come in here. What exactly are you writing about them in your article?" Monty asked.

"Well, Grayson HR has been chosen as our 'Spotlight' business this year," I replied. "We chose them as the best out of all the other privately held firms across the country. I'm here to learn what they do, how they do it, and why they're the best—if they really are the best."

"I can tell you in one word why they're successful," offered the man to my left. "They do what they say, don't over promise, and deliver what they say they will. Have for years, as long as I've known Joe."

"That's Steve French, runs an insurance agency here," said Monty. "How many years your agency been here, Steve?"

"Thirty-five," the man said proudly.

"So you've seen Grayson HR grow over the years?" I asked.

"Yes sir, we all have. Been real proud of what they've accomplished and how they help the community."

"So you'd say they do indeed walk their talk, that all their chatter about virtues is more than just fluff?"

Heads nodded around the room. It was easy to tell that every barber and customer was now focused on the topic of the morning: Grayson HR and the reporter.

"Now let me get something straight," one of the other barbers said. "How are you going to use whatever you might hear us say? Are you just looking for dirt, or the truth? Are you going to twist or quote us out of context or do any of those things we've seen reporters do?"

I love the unvarnished candor of barbershops. So refreshing in today's politically correct world. Hey, even as a veteran reporter, I get tired of all the radical nonsense from all sides of the spectrum.

"Guys, I'm here to highlight Grayson HR, to champion them as a great company; that is, if that's what they really are. My primary role is to dig behind the marketing and public relations facade to get a read on the real heart and soul of the company. I just want to know the truth, what makes them tick, and whether they walk the talk."

I paused to read the reaction. Not much so far, so I continued.

"I'm not here to expose skeletons in the Grayson HR closet or weave together rumors or false accusations to try and topple a local giant. I just want the truth. Frankly, I chose your barber shop because I knew I could get the real story here—just like where I live in Chicago—with no icing or fancy dancing."

I hoped they believed me. I meant what I said.

Tim, the barber who had spoken up first, expertly finished trimming his customer's already short hair. He lowered his arms, looked at me with a small grin and said, "OK, I think we can give you the benefit of the doubt. But if you take anything we say and twist it, we'll call your Chicago barber and tell him to scalp you."

Most of the men chuckled at that. I figured Tim was absolutely serious. No doubt there was an honor code among barbers everywhere.

"I've been a client of Grayson's for over ten years," said a man with sandy blond hair currently getting trimmed. "I'm Jason Tunks. Run a regional trucking company. Thirty-five employees. Includes office, warehouse, and drivers."

"So Jason, how did you come to be their client and what keeps you there?" I asked. "Cheap rates? Married into the family?"

Everyone laughed.

"Well, as a matter of fact, I happened to marry one of Joe Grayson's daughters," Jason said very matter-of-factly.

I blush easily. No doubt everyone could see my quickly reddening face.

"Well, I must say my size tens taste really great today," I admitted.

"No offense taken," Jason said easily. "Your name again?"

"Tony Sullivan."

"Well, Tony, yes, I married into the family, but that's not the reason I became their customer. In fact, I married Joe's daughter, Mary, five years before I bought the trucking company. That gave me a chance to learn what Joe Grayson is like as a man, a husband, a father, and a father-in-law. If my boys grow up to be just like their granddad, I'll be one proud papa."

"How so, Jason?" I was itching to set up my laptop or grab a notebook, especially in the company of such thorough fact-checkers, but I resisted.

Jason glanced around before continuing. "It all starts with Joe's personal character," he said. "Solid. Consistent. Grounded. He is a strong man of faith and lives it out loud in every aspect of his life. I've seen him in many personal situations where he could have fudged, told little white lies, or kept his own money in his pocket when people asked for some. In every case I can remember, Joe always has lived his life with integrity, honesty, generosity, and kindness. That's how he runs his business as well."

"Yeah, I've seen the same," the third barber agreed. His nametag read "Ed." "I'm a fourth generation native of Bowling Green. My parents say the same about Joe. They've known the Grayson family for several generations. Good people. Solid citizens. Good kids too. You know, Jason, you married about five levels above yourself!"

"No doubt about it, Ed" chuckled Jason. "Knew it then, and know it now."

"I can see you're all friends of Joe's," I observed. "I have to say, my first impression has been outstanding. He seems to know what he's about. But what about his business? Is it really as good as it seems at first glance? I mean, even Francis at the front desk is called the 'Director of First Impressions.' Seriously? I need to know what's really behind that facade."

Didn't think I could be any more blunt that that.

"No hype, Tony," Monty said. "What you see is the real deal." He snipped calmly around my ears as he spoke.

"That's true," said Steve. "No company is perfect, and Joe Grayson would be the first to say his is far from it. But I'd say the proof is in the pudding. Look at his employees!" A rumble of agreement sounded around the room.

"If you want to know something about a company, don't just focus on how they treat their customers. Look at how they treat their employees," Jason said. "We've all seen tyrant managers who treat their customers great but their employees awful. Joe takes great care of his people, and they'd walk through fire for him. That's a mighty loyal group."

"My daughter joined Grayson HR a little over a year ago and really loves it there," said Ed. "She works hard, and they set the bar very high for her, but I have to tell you, the work environment is fantastic. Kim knows they want to help her succeed!"

"Grayson HR is nothing short of world-class in how it recruits and retains its own staff," Steve interjected. "Even global firms like Fruit of the Loom and the management team at Corvette meet with Joe and his team regularly to learn how he builds such a great workplace. He freely shares what they do, how they do it, and how they deal with the challenges they face. That's what you call 'transparency' in today's management language, right, Tony?"

I nodded.

"That's right, Steve. That's one of the latest management trends today."

I could tell by Steve's slight grin that he was pleased to show his friends he knew something about management trends.

"Well, it might be considered a trend in Chicago, but it's here to stay in Bowling Green," Monty said. "Joe Grayson and his firm is the real deal. You can take that to the bank!"

After spinning my chair around so I could approve his work, Monty began the best part of any barber shop haircut: applying the warm lather to the back of my neck for the neck shave.

"Well, Tony," Monty said, "looks like you've got a room full of Grayson HR fans today. Is that what you expected?"

"Monty, I learned a long time ago as a reporter that expectations taint the truth, that I needed to be totally open to wherever the truth took me. Looks like the truth took me right into your chair."

"Too bad it didn't take you into mine." said Ed. "I'm a much better barber than Monty."

"Maybe next time, Ed," I chuckled.

As Monty wiped my neck with the hot towel and carefully removed the cape, I handed him $20 and told him to keep the change, even though his sign clearly said a cut and lather was only $12. He thanked me sincerely, and invited me back for more research any time.

Steve and I left the shop together, and I paused to admire the scenery outside the shop. The image of tall shade trees and clean sidewalks on both sides of the street spoke of quiet peace and stability. I could see a corner of the town square with a handful of shoppers and businesspeople strolling by on their way to the next shop or appointment. Just like I remembered during my college days here.

"You know, Tony, I remembered something else," Steve mentioned just before we parted ways. "I noticed you looking around here—we take a lot of pride in our downtown. There's something else you should know about Joe Grayson, and I didn't want to say it in front of everybody else inside. It's something he doesn't want everybody knowing."

This was what I was looking for! Finally, I reached into my pocket and extracted my notebook.

"Oh really? I'd love to know more."

Steve indicated a bench just down the street, out of sight of the barber shop. We sat down together.

"When Joe Grayson first picked the location for his business, it was a pretty major construction job for that neighborhood. There were hearings, rezoning meetings, everything. There were some existing businesses on the street that weren't too happy about all the construction traffic and noise. My sister has a little restaurant over that way and she was pretty sure it would hurt her business, with the parking limited and all.

"But I'll tell you what–Joe Grayson stopped by her restaurant and talked with her personally. Asked her what he could do to be a good neighbor–give the restaurant a new sign, a new paint job, landscaping, whatever.

"You could've knocked my sister over with a feather," Steve continued. "Nobody expected Joe Grayson to do anything like that! And he kept his word–hired a company to create a new sign to her specifications, and then brought in a landscape designer and crew to really brighten up the outside of the restaurant. Even built one of those little garbanzo things out back for people to sit outside and eat."

I diligently fought the mental image of a large, pale bean perched behind the restaurant, knowing Steve meant "gazebo," not "garbanzo." Good thing we'd left the barber shop, right?

"Joe paid for the whole thing himself–and stopped back in again when it was done to make sure my sister was happy," Steve concluded. "Only thing he asked was that she not make all this common knowledge–he said it was just being a good neighbor, and he wasn't in it for the publicity."

I nodded thoughtfully.

"By chance is your sister's name Mary?" I asked. Steve brightened.

"It is! Have you met her?"

"Let's just say she doesn't lie about that pie of hers," I said with a broad grin.

"Yep—you've met Mary," Steve laughed.

Just when I thought I was getting the dirt on Grayson HR, it seemed Joe Grayson had even beat me to the dirt—and landscaped it!

It was good to know that in America there were still places that updated their look, but retained their character. Bowling Green was one. In many ways it was the same town I'd loved as a college student, but it was clearly bigger and better than when I'd lived here. It had aged graciously, and still remained a great, dynamic mid-American college town. A place I was proud to call "home." Go Big Red!

Chapter 13

THE EXIT INTERVIEW

"So tell me what you've learned, Tony. I want to hear the unvarnished truth."

Once again I faced Joe in his office, and this time he was the one asking the questions.

As I summarized the people I'd interviewed, what I'd learned about Grayson HR's various virtues and how they were implemented, and how I confirmed my observations at the barbershop, I could tell Joe was pleased but not ecstatic.

"I appreciate your insights, Tony. But what I'd really like to know is what you've found out about our flaws, what we need to be doing better. That's the only way we can improve."

I nodded. "I admire your desire to know the truth," I told Joe. Here's what I'm seeing. Everyone from your employees to your customers to your community seems to understand what you and Grayson HR stand for. They know it all starts with your first virtue, character. You and your team are sincere in living all four of your virtues. You don't force these values on anyone, but when your employees see it lived out loud, they buy in—drink your Kool-Aid, if you will."

"You have a simple but effective model for running your business, and also your life. You back it up with real-world teeth, like your support of the assisted living facility going through a leveraged buy out."

"But?" Joe was smiling, but his eyes were serious. I shrugged, never liking to be the bearer of bad news.

Pulling out my notebook and opening it to a clean page, I began making a list of words.

#1. Clarity

#2. Leverage

#3. Execution

#4. Impact

"From my years at Lens Shift, I've learned that the best companies are without exception extremely clear on who they are, who they serve, and where they're going. They ask, and answer, these kinds of questions very well:

What are our core values, or as you say, our convictions?

What is our purpose?

What is, to use your phrase, our Point of Dominance?

What is our brand, our customer promise?

What are our strategic priorities over the next three years?

What key numbers must we hit, be they financial, operational, or personal?

How will we celebrate our successes and failures?

Joe studied my list for a moment. He retrieved his own notebook from his desk and began making notes. I could see he was thinking things over before speaking.

"Tony, these are excellent questions. I can see where we can put them to work here immediately to help us strengthen our clarity. Now, tell me about leverage. What does that mean?"

"Leverage is how you maximize both your organizational and people strengths. I've learned that sustained greatness depends on simultaneously maximizing your strengths and making your weaknesses irrelevant. Same thing applies to every employee. You can have a great organizational culture with lots of clarity, but if people are in roles or jobs that don't maximize their strengths, the entire system suffers. It's critical that both system and individual strengths line up with the goals of the firm established in the 'clarity' discussions."

"That's something I've struggled with, Tony, for a long time. Am I really taking advantage of all the opportunities God opens for us, and am I allowing our people to really excel?" Joe jotted a few more notes, then leaned back and templed his fingers, something I realized he did when he was really concentrating.

I pointed to the next word on my list.

"Execution is the system or systems that move you toward meeting goals and priorities. One of the main differences between good companies and excellent ones is how they develop and measure their execution methods." I studied Joe for a moment. "I'm sure you measure performance here, but I'd like to know more about how you drive goal execution and hold your people a accountable for the results."

Joe was silent. Having learned through the years that one of the most powerful tools in anyone's communication arsenal is silence, I let the silence hang in the room. Often I learned more about someone by remaining silent and allowing them to struggle with their thoughts than in asking a series of rapid-fire questions.

Finally, Joe admitted, "This is an area where I'm not doing well. Yes, we have terrific results. But it seems to me that my personal strength is in creating a vision and a culture that drives our convictions. I am not strong in measurement and holding our people accountable. That's a weakness that I need to make irrelevant. No doubt about it, this is an area we must improve right away." I could see the determination in his face.

"Don't beat yourself up too much, Joe," I said. "This is one of the most common shortcomings I've seen in most growth-oriented firms. The great news is, it's fixable!"

Again, Joe jotted down some notes in his journal.

"And what else do you see in those firms?" he asked.

"Well, I find the best firms focus on what I call 'impact.'" I gently closed the cover of Joe's journal long enough to reveal the words "Impact Journal" embossed on the cover. "Interesting that your journal has the same word. Typically, I see successful firms focus on at least one of four impact categories.

"Colleagues—fellow employees.

"Customers—those who pay the bills.

"Constituents—vendors, suppliers, not direct customers.

"Community—those who live and work in surrounding geographical areas, including government, private, and social groups.

"In my reporting I call this the 4C's," I continued. "I expect this acronym would fit in well with all the others you have floating around Grayson HR."

Joe was writing quickly. "Yes it would, Tony. Do you mind if we use your 4C model around here?"

"Only if I get a piece of any residuals," I chuckled.

Joe laughed, but then his expression turned serious again. "Tony, we may be doing some things well, but through your eyes I can see we have a long way to go. In fact, I'm not so sure we deserve to be your Spotlight company."

"I would respectfully disagree with that, Joe," I replied. "In fact, that's precisely the quality that confirms to me that you're exactly the right choice for our Spotlight feature this year. You're not resting on your laurels. Every great firm that desires to remain great has a passion to take their business and their team to a higher level of success and significance. That describes both you and Grayson HR."

Joe set his pen down and nodded slowly. "Thank you, Tony. That observation means a lot. And thank you for sharing your four steps with me. You've given me a lot to work on and improve." By the expression on his face, I could see the wheels already turning. Joe Grayson was a man on a mission!

It was clear Joe was ready to wrap up the interview and get to work. I employed a tried and true reporter's technique.

"Joe...just one more thing?"

Chapter 14

THE IMPACT 500

"You and the entire Grayson HR team make a big deal about being a company that bases all it does on the Bible," I began. "That seems a bit radical to me, especially in the dog-eat-dog world of business. Doesn't that place unnecessary additional burdens on you and your team?"

Braced for a trick question, Joe seemed to relax. "It's just the opposite, Tony. In fact, it's a blessing, not a burden. And there might be more of us than you think."

I decided to run at this another way. "But you must admit most private businesses aren't run on the Bible. That would certainly make Grayson HR part of a minority, right?"

"Depends on how you define minority."

I wasn't inclined to dance around what was potentially a tough issue.

"OK, Joe, I'll grant you that a few top firms claim to run on Biblical principles. Hobby Lobby, Chick-Fil-A, Interstate Battery, In-N-Out Burgers and Service Master come to mind. But these firms are small potatoes in the big scheme of things, right?

"Like I said, it depends," Joe replied. He pulled my notebook to him and flipped to a blank page. "There are around 5.4 million privately held, for-profit firms with under 500 employees in the United States. In addition, research suggests at least 75% of Americans claim to be Christians. They may not be practicing Christians, they may be just professing Christians, Christians in name only but not in their actions. So this means there are 4.1 million privately held firms with under 500 employees all across America with at least one professing, and perhaps practicing, Christian working there. Following me so far?"

I studied the numbers jotted on the page.

"Got it. Continue."

"Conservatively, let's say that only two percent of those 4.1 million firms, just two percent, have a leader or maybe two that are the real deal; they sincerely want to honor God in their work." Joe's gaze was intense. "You mentioned some really big firms a minute ago, each one with far more than 500 employees. I'm not including them. Would you say that two percent of the rest is a conservative number?"

"Mathematically, yes," I admitted. Where on earth was Joe going? I was supposed to be asking the questions!

"Now, do the math: two percent of 4.1 million firms is how many firms, Tony?"

"Well, over 70,000 I'd guess." I cleared my throat, resisting the urge to use my phone's calculator app. Math was not my best subject in school. Another good reason I worked with words for a living.

"Good guess!" Joe agreed. He continued writing on my notepad. "88,500, to be more specific. Here is what all this means, Tony. Conservatively, there is a minimum of 88,500 for-profit, privately held firms in America whose leaders desire to make an impact for God through their work. That does not mean they run around preaching to everyone. Far from it. Some of them quietly support foundations or missions that evangelize. We do. But that's not necessarily their primary purpose, although critically important.

"Think about this and Lens Shift. There's great potential 'leadership readership' for you—in this pocket of companies whose leaders are doing business a different way. They're competitive, profit-producing firms just like us that use the Bible as their foundational management book. That's 88,500 companies." Joe underlined that number in my notebook. "Even if they average only ten employees, that's almost a million potential Lens Shift readers right there."

"I can see future story potential here," I said thoughtfully. "But are they really having an impact?"

"Individually, yes, they are having an impact," Joe said. "Collectively, not as much. That's why I'm so excited about an organization called The Impact 500."

"The Impact 500?" I frowned. "Is that some type of NAS-CAR event?"

Joe laughed.

"The Impact 500 is a hub, a connection point if you will, for businesses like mine," he explained. "It's a place for 2%ers, that's what we call ourselves, to share success stories, challenges, best practices, and collective wisdom. That means we share our mistakes so others don't make the same bonehead decisions. I've got a file cabinet full of these!" He pointed to a file behind his desk.

I was impressed. "A group that shares lessons learned the hard way? That's hard to believe, Joe. Some companies depend on their competitors making the same mistakes they once did!"

Joe nodded eagerly. "Believe it, Tony. I'm a member of the Impact 500 Board of Directors, and I'm really enjoying the opportunity to build this network. We're sure that if we can connect and share biblically-based business excellence with each other, together we can impact eternity."

"Thanks for telling me about them," I said, jotting "The Impact 500" in my notebook and making a note to Google them to learn more.

"Care to come to one of our events?" Joe asked. "Our next conference happens to be right here in Bowling Green, and it's just four weeks away. It's a one-day event with several speakers and breakout sessions. I'll be the opening speaker and sharing Grayson HR's story. We've got over 600 registrants so far. Is that something Lens Shift would want to cover? Maybe for future stories?"

I pursed my lips thoughtfully. "I'll take that up with my boss," I said. "My first priority is getting this story submitted and approved, though."

"I'll pray about that, Tony." Joe flipped to another section in his journal and made a note.

Without meaning to, I snorted. "That's something I don't hear every day."

"I'll bet you don't," Joe said. "Around here, we mean it. We pray about stuff every day. Prayed about your visit, even whether to accept the invitation to be highlighted. We really don't like to bring attention to ourselves. There's a fine line between marketing and bragging. The Bible teaches to let others brag on you, not you yourself or you become prideful."

"I don't sense a lot of that around here. Pride in your company, yes. Esprit d'corps. But not personal pride."

Joe rubbed his chin thoughtfully. "Don't be fooled, Tony. We're human, no better, no worse. We fight the same fights everyone else does. We just take a somewhat different approach."

"No doubt," I admitted. "I admire your approach, and your financial success is just one measure of your impact."

"Well, we're for-profit, and only through making a profit can we continue. I'm not the least bit ashamed of it. But as you see, we strive to do much more around here than just meet quarterly earnings forecasts. It's really about eternity."

"Eternity?" I know Joe sensed my skepticism. Was he intentionally laying it on a little thick for purposes of the interview and the story?

Joe's expression was earnest as he continued. "Ultimately, everything we do in this life determines where we'll spend eternity. Not everyone believes that, or at least they say they don't. But down deep, everyone knows that this life isn't all there is. There's more. We will live on somewhere. And the only things we carry into eternity are our character and our relationships. Our hope here is to influence and 'grow' people's character in such a way that they develop a relationship now with Jesus. Yeah, that is so politically incorrect, but that's what we believe."

Joe leaned in, lowered his voice, and said, "Tony, I hope the same for you–that you will just consider developing a relationship with Jesus."

Evidently Joe had also mastered the use of silence. He paused, and I–the writer, the wordsmith–had no words.

"There's one more thing," Joe continued. "Whether you know it or not, I'm sure there are people around you, perhaps even in your inner circle of friends or colleagues, who are 2%ers themselves. Their companies may not be, but they belong to the two percent club in that they want to make an impact for God in their own workplace. Open your eyes to the possibility, Tony. You might be surprised at how many there are and how close they are to you. All it takes is a Lens Shift."

I tucked my notebook away. "Well said, Joe. I'll try out this new lens you suggest and see what it reveals. On both fronts, for me and with my colleagues. I promise."

Joe leaned back with a broad grin. "Thanks. I know you mean that. Your character is showing, as our character always does. Keep me posted on what you discover. Confidentially, of course." He handed me a small card. "Here is my personal G-Mail. No need for anyone around here to see it. "

I accepted the card. "Thank you. Again, I will."

"My cell number is on there too," Joe pointed out. "All my employees and customers have it. Might as well let you have it too," he said with a wink.

"Appreciate it." Nice gesture, but I was betting that cell number was a burner phone, not Joe's personal one. The proof would be in the pudding, and I resolved to call it later and see whether it went directly to voice mail or whether I reached Joe himself.

Joe was quicker on the draw than I expected.

"Can I borrow your phone for a second?"

Somewhat reluctantly, I handed it over. He dialed a number. The phone in Joe's pocket immediately began ringing. I was impressed.

"Just in case you were thinking I wasn't serious," he said, handing my phone back to me. "And Tony…I hope you'll think seriously about taking your relationship with Jesus to a higher level."

Over the years, I've been yelled at, threatened, intimidated and even shunned by so-called "loving Christians" who insist I need to believe what they believe or face expulsion by God. Yet in my experience, no one has moved me so powerfully as Joe did with his suggestion that I simply think about it.

Just think about it, he says? Anyone can do that.

"Thanks, Joe. I will."

"Good." Joe stood up. "Call me if you have any questions about the article or about your journey into eternity. I may not have all the answers, but we can work on it together."

This man is indeed 'The Impacter,' I realize. He's left quite a mark on me in just two days. Maybe a mark that will last into eternity?

Chapter 15

THE DISCOVERY

O ne of the great truisms known to all writers is: Writers
don't write–they rewrite! We learn, either by experience,
education or both, that we must throw our ideas on paper (or on
a digital screen these days), let them marinate in our brains, and
aggressively reorder, rearrange, reassess, regurgitate, and generally
rewrite everything we initially compose.

During my flight back to Chicago, as I began transcribing
my notes and recapturing my impressions onto my computer,
something unusual struck me, something that hadn't happened
with any previous assignment I could ever recall. Reflecting on
Grayson HR, I was left with an almost palpable sense of peace.

I couldn't recall any other investigative story where I left
without even an iota of suspicion or even disgust after my initial
interview. Instead, my typical cynicism had been replaced with a
quiet peace, leaving me surprised and more than a little confused.

The in-flight bell signaled our approach to the airport, and
the flight attendants made their required announcements. I

tucked my Mac into my bag and shoved it under the seat in front of me. A text from Liz alerted me to the fact that Bart was expecting a draft of the article by noon the next day. It looked like a long night ahead.

The hours flew by as I transcribed notes, wrote, edited, rewrote, wrestled with words and phrases, and considered how best to frame the article. Finally, when the thoughts were coming together, I took some time to check some facts and figures. That's when I made a startling discovery.

Joe's story did not begin with Grayson HR. Turns out his happily-ever-after didn't begin with "once upon a time in Bowling Green."

Further research uncovered more than just a hint of scandal. Joe had failed miserably in a previous business. He'd been implicated in some very unethical dealings. While never indicted, during his time serving as CFO of a well-known financial institution, there were accusations of inappropriate conduct. He'd stepped down quickly—for "health reasons?" Really? I continued researching.

His wife had left him. Some very unflattering interviews were given, interviews where he was the subject, but was never consulted directly. He'd left his home and...low and behold...was that one of those dreaded "gaps" on his resume? Joe had a couple of years he couldn't account for? I checked, but he didn't seem to have a criminal record. No time served. Exactly who was Joe Grayson, anyway?

This wasn't something I could just overlook. I wrestled with the information for an hour or so, looking at two different article drafts. One included Joe's back story. One didn't. Which was the right one to submit to Bart? And should I talk with Joe before making the decision? I knew his cell number was already stored in my phone. What to do?

I arrived at the office a few minutes before noon the next day, running on fumes and a full pot of black coffee. Liz was at her desk, and when she saw me approaching, she smiled broadly.

"Does Bart have a few minutes this afternoon for me?" I asked gingerly.

"Are you kidding? Your article is A-1 on his list today." She glanced at his closed office door. "But I think he's at lunch right now. Can you come back in thirty minutes?"

"You bet."

I took the stairs down to the first floor sandwich shop, grabbed a roast beef on wheat and some yogurt, and then scurried back to my office, grabbing a cup of coffee (decaf!) from our break room along the way. Sitting down at my desk, I booted up my Mac to catch up on emails, including Bart's next assignment list.

I was surprised to see Liz approaching my desk a few minutes later. She looked almost apologetic for interrupting me.

"Tony, got a minute?" she asked. I indicated the chair next to my desk, chewing quickly to swallow a big bite of sandwich.

"I hope you'll forgive me, but Bart forwarded a draft of your article to me and asked me to take a look," she said. "All I can say is, what a company! Grayson HR sounds like a great place to work!" Liz paused. "What really caught my attention was when you said that Joe suggests 2%ers are everywhere. Would you agree?"

"Not sure, Liz," I admitted. "I never really looked for them before."

Then it hit me. The way Joe and his team approached their work was exactly the way Liz approached her work. With character. Competence. Courage. Commitment. She quietly displayed these very same virtues right here at Lens Shift. Could it be…?

Liz was a 2%er!

A smile spread slowly across Liz's face as she studied mine, knowing I was connecting the dots. I said, "Liz, living these four virtues out loud is what makes you different, isn't it?"

She nodded.

"So tell me, Liz. Why haven't I been able to see this before?"

"Tony, although I've been a believer for over twenty years, only in the last three years or so have I taken to heart what the Bible says about work and how I should approach it. I'm not an 'in-your-face' believer, wearing a fish symbol or hitting you over the head with verses. Far from it. I've learned that for me, the best way to show my faith is to walk it. What Joe calls 'integrity.'"

"It's easy to overlook," Liz went on, "especially when you're not looking for it in the first place. Even more so for those of us who don't wear our faith on our sleeve. But hearing you say this about me is both reassuring and unsettling."

"What do you mean?" I asked.

"It's reassuring that you see these virtues in my work around here. That's good. But it's unsettling to me that I haven't had the courage to be a little bit bolder in who I am and how it makes a difference in what I do here. I guess even we 2%ers struggle with living these virtues out loud. You've inspired me to pray about how to be a little more transparent without turning people off."

"I wish other believers felt the same," I said. "Seems to me a lot of them are really pushy and, frankly, arrogant."

"That's a real shame," Liz agreed. "Those pushy ones annoy me, too. They are truly the minority of believers. You can see that now just being around Joe's team. I'll bet few if any people there were pushy or aggressive toward you."

"Just the opposite," I said. "That's probably why I listened to their side—I mean, your side."

"I'm really proud that you didn't avoid the faith issue in this article," Liz said.

"I couldn't. It's too deeply ingrained in their culture, or should I say their corporate character. I would be doing them a disservice to dismiss something that's so important to them, whether I agree with it or not. That's poor journalistic standards."

"Sure wish more in our industry thought the same."

"So, Liz, I'm curious. You've worked with Bart as long as I have. What's his take on the article?"

"You might be surprised." Liz stood up.

"Meaning?"

"You'll know in a few minutes."

I glanced at my watch. 1:25. Bart does not tolerate being even one minute late for a meeting or appointment. He says it steals other people's time and is very rude.

When I got back to his office, Bart's door was open and he invited me to come in. He wasted no time on small talk.

Leaning back in his chair, Bart looked straight at me. "Think Grayson is the real deal, or are they just a big facade?"

I held his gaze.

"They are the real deal."

"Coming from you, Tony, that's quite a statement. With your background and all the shenanigans you've covered, if anyone on my staff can spot a phony business, you can."

"I take that as a compliment." Bart didn't hand out praise easily, and I was surprised—and a little suspicious. "So, what do you want to change in the article?"

"Not a thing."

I frowned. I'd never heard that in all my years. Editors edit. Writers rewrite.

"I've already sent it to the editing staff with a STAT order."

I couldn't have heard him correctly.

"Bart, in all my years here, I've never heard you tell any of your staff reporters that it's good enough as is. You're great at finding missing thoughts, non-supported conclusions, and even erroneous stats. You mean to tell me you didn't find anything in my article that needed revising or at least re-checking?"

Bart let his silence speak for a few seconds. Then he spoke. "Tony, for whatever the reason, you gave Grayson HR the benefit of the doubt, allowing them to share candidly about their virtues and how they lived them, without using the typical lenses of arrogance, self-righteousness, and disbelief. The article is a fair, objective, and reasonable representation of their company. No cheap shots. No judgments. Just their story on how they use a biblical lens or model for their business. I didn't need to do anything with that."

I studied Bart curiously. "I can tell something's on your mind, Bart. What is it?"

"Have you talked to Liz at all about this article?"

"Just now. She's a 2%er. Now that I know what that means, it's obvious."

Bart paused again. Once again I began connecting the dots.

"And Bart…are you also a 2%er?"

How could I have missed that?

Bart's voice was a little gruff when he spoke. "I've got a long way to go, Tony, but I want to lead this company just like Joe Grayson leads his. Your story inspired me to take a closer look at what I do, how I lead, and how I can better align it with the wisdom of the Bible. Does that shock you?"

I shook my head. "Before this interview with Grayson HR, I would have been disgusted with even the thought of it. Probably would have considered resigning on the spot. But now, even as a non-believer, I can see what it means to be a 2%er in business and the impact it can have. I understand why that is important to you. And I've learned that when it's done right, no one, not even atheists, would be offended in working in such a company or with such good people."

Bart leaned forward. "So, Tony, what would you think if we at Lens Shift started clarifying our values and holding people here more accountable to them?

"No brainer, Bart. It would make a difference. It would have an impact."

Bart grinned. "And what if I confessed, or at least admitted, to others that I am an emerging 2%er. How do you think that would go over?"

I was honest. "Before this article, like a lead balloon. After this article, at least you have a foundation from which to begin the discussion."

"Fair enough."

Just before leaving the office, I remembered something else Joe had said.

"Bart, one more thing. Joe said he would be a speaker in a few weeks at The Impact 500 event in Bowling Green I mentioned in the article. He invited me to attend. I was wondering if maybe I could attend? I'll even take some leave time and go at my own expense."

Bart flipped open a page in his notebook. "I'll fly down with you. I'll ask Liz to book our tickets."

Bart leaving the office? Unbelievable. How could one visit to one company on one story impact me, my boss, his assistant, and perhaps my entire company?

Chapter 16

THE ARTICLE

The Impacter Strikes Again

By Tony Sullivan
LENS SHIFT Magazine

In this economy, there's an unspoken sense that ANY job is a great job. However, employees have never been more outspoken with their complaints and general dissatisfaction, regardless of their occupation or organization. If it's true that any job is a great job, then why does it matter where we work?

Because for most people, their work becomes more than just a mindless job. "Having an identity you're proud of is important," says Carlin Flora, author of *Friendfluence: The Surprising Ways Friends Make Us Who We Are.* "Your career needs to reflect the 'real you'—otherwise even if it seems promising, it probably won't make you happy."

Companies are realizing that in order to not only survive, but also thrive, they need to recognize their employees as whole people, not just as what they can do for the company and its bottom line.

Who's doing it right?

Lens Shift has selected Grayson Human Resources, headquartered in Bowling Green, Kentucky, as its "Spotlight" company for this year. With 16 consecutive years of sales growth, Grayson HR is definitely a leader in the field of human resources. In an industry where turnover is not only a possibility, but also a constant reality, Grayson HR enjoys one of the lowest attrition rates in the business. They attract top people who want to stay and grow with the company. What is Grayson HR doing right?

Believe it or not, Grayson HR began as the product of years of dissatisfaction, culminating in two lists. "Stupid Things I've Seen Leaders Do" and "What Leaders Need to Be" were the driving force behind founder and CEO Joe Grayson's vision for doing what he already knew how to do, but in a totally unconventional way.

Virtues, not Values

"Virtues are people's guiding principles, special moral qualities of excellence that come from deep inside and are lived out in daily activities," says Grayson. His four key virtues: Character, Competence, Courage, and Commitment.

Character: depth of moral convictions.

- Wisdom (knowing what's right)
- Integrity (doing what's right)
- Self Discipline (keep doing what's right even when it's tough)

"Your character is revealed not so much by what you believe, but by what you do, especially when it costs you something," says Sally Metz, Grayson HR's Director of Worker's Compensation. "For example, as a leader you know the right thing to do is pay your suppliers within 30 days of their invoice. Let's say we're having a cash flow crunch, and we decide we can't pay within 30 days, so we wait 45 days, or even 60 days, to pay. Our integrity comes into play, and from our suppliers' perspective, our character. Some companies just say, 'Hey, that's business.' At Grayson, we see it as much more. It's a reflection of our character."

Grayson HR's commitment to character means the company sees its clients and its employees as whole people – not just what they can do for the company. In particular, Grayson is committed to employee wellness. Beyond the health care premium contributions it makes on behalf of not just the employee, but also their dependents, the company offers incentives for participating in employee wellness programs. Grayson employees and their families are encouraged to use a state-of-the-art, on-site fitness center, and Grayson even subsidizes the use of off-site fitness centers when that's a more convenient option for some. The company has arranged discounts at local restaurants serving healthy meal options. Grayson HR is field testing a new program called "wellness coaching" within its ranks, allowing employees private access to financial counseling, grief support, and event planning services. People are more than just the sum total of their job skills and experience, and Grayson HR not only gets this...it encourages it.

Competence: depth of skills/abilities.
- Envision (strategy–what's next)
- Engage (people–who needs to be involved in what's next)
- Execute (results–how and when to launch)

"What separates Grayson from 98% of other firms in the industry is that we base everything on our corporate character. It's not about success, though that is important. It's about significance," says Dave Justin, Grayson HR's Workplace Safety Director. "Grayson is dedicated to moving beyond success to significance. Instead of a traditional business focusing on profit, prestige, and power, we take it to a higher level, where we focus our efforts on purpose, principles and people."

Grayson HR leads the pack when it comes to employee development. Joe Grayson is a firm believer in "pushing the envelope," always vetting his people for leadership. It's a two-pronged approach: Grayson employees develop the skills they need for the jobs they're doing today, and they're being trained for the jobs they'll do tomorrow. Performance reviews are coupled with career action plans, and workshops encouraging people to strategize about career development are widely advertised and well attended. Mentor relationships are common, as are departmental rotations and leadership shadowing opportunities.

"The real power of our approach is that we take the same model into all levels of the organization. It's not just for senior leadership. It applies across the board, so we're all working from the same playbook," says Rebecca Godfrey, Director of People.

Courage: the willingness to act on your convictions.
- Confidence
- Composure
- Boldness

Billy Linville, Grayson HR's Director of Benefits, experienced Grayson HR's unique definition of courage firsthand when he was diagnosed with cancer seven years ago. "The diagnosis was profound, to say the least," says Linville. "I read and learned all I could. I envisioned the result—a life free of cancer (confidence). I enlisted help from experts and other sources (composure). I developed and began executing a plan (boldness). As my confidence grew, so did my composure to face whatever was ahead."

Seven years later, Linville has been declared cancer-free. He now leads Cancer Freedom Day: An Alternative Approach seminars, featuring company-wide workshops, organic food lunches, and giveaways to attendees.

Commitment: dedicated to a long-term course of action.
- Purpose (why do you want to do this?)
- Payoff (end result or goal)
- Perseverance (persisting when times are tough/uncertain)

Grayson HR Business Development Consultant Laney Tabor's job is a mix of sales, marketing, and customer development. In her position, she has opportunities to demonstrate the company's commitment to its clients. ABC Assisted Living Center experienced an unexpected action by its parent company. Finding themselves on the market, the ABC management team decided to attempt a leveraged buyout. With so much of their cash flow and capital tied up in legal fees and negotiations, they began falling behind in their payments. The business relationship was in jeopardy.

Knowing the value of their business through the years, and the potential for keeping their business in years to come, Grayson HR worked closely with ABC to revise their existing contract, negotiate special repayment terms, and offer employee support like human resource and payroll experts during the transition. "ABC knew we were there for them for the long term, regardless of the outcome," says Tabor. "Our commitment to them was so obvious and profound, we knew they would be one of our most vocal allies within their industry. That's more valuable and meaningful than any marketing or sales campaign."

Going Global

Grayson HR understands the importance of not only surviving, but also thriving, in multiple markets. Access to offsite work tools reduces the need for travel and opens up opportunities to connect and collaborate. Alternative leadership programs give high-performing leaders opportunities to work in another country for nine months to a year. In this way, multi-cultural, multi-functional teams work together to achieve a goal or solve a problem, with uncommon results.

It's character, not culture

"We don't focus on corporate culture. We focus on corporate character," says Grayson. "To me, 'corporate culture' is a very vague and meaningless concept. It's impersonal, difficult to measure, demands little personal control or accountability, and is externally prompted by means of compliance—what we have to do or be. In a sense, it's 'going through the motions' while things are all messed up underneath.

"Instead, we emphasize corporate character. It's personal, easy to measure, offers total personal control, inspires excellence, and focuses on who we are and want to become. It's taking responsibility for your own actions and reactions, regardless of the culture around you. It's about character—about who you are in the dark, when no one's looking and everyone's compromising."

CORPORATE CULTURE	CORPORATE CHARACTER
Impersonal (they, them)	Personal (me/mine)
Hard to measure	Easy to measure
Little personal control	Total personal control
Forces compliance	Inspires excellence
What we must do/obey	Who we are/must become

Interesting words coming from a man who has lived them. Joe Grayson knows something about compromise. Not so long ago, Grayson had it all. He was CFO of an internationally known financial institution. He was leading the way in an industry that seemed to have unlimited potential.

Then something happened. Grayson stepped down abruptly, for reasons known only to him. And he disappeared from the radar screen of the business world. For two years, Joe Grayson was off the grid. No LinkedIn profile. No Facebook posts. No tweets. No e-mails. No speaking engagements. No public appearances. Nothing.

And then, two years later, a small human resources compendium appeared in Bowling Green, Kentucky, Grayson's hometown. Though it didn't cover a large geographical area or a significant share of the human resources market, this company was refreshingly different. It began to grow, and thrive, but not through traditional channels. It didn't go after big clients or generate splashy, attention-getting headlines. In fact, the company and its employees seemed content to stay...well...small-town.

But something else was at work within the walls of Grayson HR. Word of the small firm with the fresh perspective began to spread. Instead of going after new clients, new clients began seeking them out. The company began to grow. They began attracting talented employees from bigger, well-known firms in cities around the world. Instead of being one of the pack, Grayson HR began leading the way.

A Company of Character

"When we can release the human spirit at work, we're tapping into something great." says Grayson. "We are releasing the passion, the energy, the latent potential we believe God gives everyone, even those who haven't chosen to personally follow Him."

Is all this too good to be true? We all know the old adage, "You can fool all of the people some of the time, and some of the people all of the time..." So many organizations can fool us for a while, even those once featured as Lens Shift "Spotlight" companies. We've chosen firms like Enron and Lehman Brothers as the best in their day, and cringed when they fell. We've heralded up-

and-coming leaders like Jim Bakker and Ted Haggard for their vision and ethics. We've witnessed the special contempt reserved for so-called faithful servants of God when they fall from their glorious pedestals.

In light of this, there are still many questions to answer about Grayson's past before we can confirm that Grayson HR is indeed the real deal, or just a so-far successful attempt to mask past missteps.

Grayson is convinced his company's emphasis on virtues and character over culture sets them apart. Not satisfied with building on his current success, he's pushing forward with a new venture. The Impact 500 (see below) is moving Grayson HR to a higher level. "We know if we can connect and share biblically-based business excellence with each other, together we can impact eternity in a big way," Grayson says.

Will this happen? Only time will tell. Maybe Grayson's real character—and the character of his company—will finally shine through. When it does, Lens Shift will be there.

Chapter 17

RETURN TO BOWLING GREEN

Bart agreed that 'The Impacter Strikes Again' was the right title for the article. It went to press later that week and the 'Spotlight' issue shipped just three weeks after my meetings with Bart and Liz.

Initial sales data indicated this could be the biggest selling 'Spotlight' issue in our history. Our Lens Shift social media team did a fantastic job blasting Tweets, Facebook posts, blogs, and national radio and TV business show interviews, as well as driving non-print buyers to our digital magazine.

Could the initial sales spike be due to the incredible media buzz we created, the story itself, or maybe both? Time would tell, but my sense was 'both.'

The return flight to Nashville and the drive to Bowling Green gave Bart and me a chance to just talk, without deadlines, interruptions, or pressing problems. He shared his personal journey to finally admitting he was a 2%er, how he became a believer years ago, and his fears along the way of being scorned, outcast, or even fired for his beliefs.

His candor took guts, what Joe would call courage, and I admired him for it.

Later, settling into my hotel room, I flipped through the television channels, trying to find something to distract me from the thoughts racing through my mind. I could sleep anywhere; it wasn't the unfamiliar surroundings, or the coffee, or the conversation with Bart. What was it that my mind couldn't seem to resolve?

It wasn't my mind. It was my heart, and I knew exactly what the problem was. I hadn't heard a word from Joe Grayson, or anyone at Grayson HR, since the article had run. Did they see me as a hard-bitten reporter leaving no stone unturned in his zeal to uncover the whole truth? Or did they see me as a traitor in their midst, polite to their faces in an effort to undermine all they'd accomplished with Joe at the helm? Had I done the right thing, submitted the right draft, told the story in the right way at the right time to the right audience? Or had I crossed the sometimes-blurry line of ethical reporting?

And why on earth was this even bothering me? Was this an attack of conscience? As a reporter, I had to pursue the facts and act on them quickly, whether I liked them or not. My career depended on the instincts I now seemed to be questioning.

Chapter 18

THE CONFERENCE

As the hotel elevator doors opened onto the conference floor, I could see The Impact 500 registration table was abuzz, with at least four people deep in five separate lines. I joined the people waiting to sign in.

When I reached the front of the line and gave my name, a very efficient woman scanned the list once…twice…and then looked confused. Apparently my name was not on the general registration list. Had Liz somehow dropped the ball? Did she overlook getting us registered? Maybe we owed the conference fee? I couldn't imagine Liz doing any of those things.

The woman at the registration table spoke quietly into her headset, and another woman approached, with another list. There my name was, listed under the guests at "Table 2." I also spotted Bart's name on the same list.

"Mr. Sullivan, you'll be sitting at table two as a special guest of Mr. Grayson. I hope that's okay with you?"

I was surprised and pleased. "Absolutely. Thank you very much."

She handed me the a conference brochure, a small satchel for handouts and flyers, and a beautiful black leather-bound journal embossed with "Impact Journal." Just like Joe's, I recalled. As a professional writer, I've used and seen just about every style of journal on the market. This one seemed exceptionally nice.

Why would I expect anything less?

As I entered the conference room and made my way toward my table, I was amazed to see several business leaders I'd met through my assignments at Lens Shift. Everyone who recognized me gave me a warm, friendly welcome, not the typical response to an investigative reporter, even though some of my articles about their companies were less than flattering. These executives and business owners introduced me to their colleagues as a great journalist and encouraged everyone to read my articles in Lens Shift magazine. Some of the people I met even recognized my name and had read my work. Several asked if I was here to do another story. I was pleased to tell them we were considering more stories on 2%er firms and their impact.

Making my way to my seat, I spotted Joe Grayson. Unsure of the reception I'd be getting from him after the article went out, I was astonished when he greeted me with a huge grin and a bear hug.

"I'm so glad you're here, Tony! Your article is sure generating a lot of 'buzz' around this place! I'm praying this conference helps you gain insight on not only how we 2%ers do business, but much more important, on how to answer your questions on your own life. And I know as a top notch reporter, you're already asking yourself some questions."

"Yes I am, Joe," I admitted, though I hadn't really realized that before now. "I'm here to look at things through the Impact 500 lens, and we'll see what happens next. By the way, I have the signed copy of the Lens Shift issue I promised Francis. Thought I would ask you to personally deliver it rather than just mail it. Seems like that would be the Grayson HR approach, wouldn't you say?"

Joe beamed. "It would indeed, Tony. In fact, you can give it to her today. She'll be here at lunch to join us."

"That's great!" I said enthusiastically. "And Joe? Just one more thing." We both chuckled. "Bart and I would like to present a special framed cover to you and the entire Grayson HR team. Bart has that one, and he can tell you a little later what your story and this conference means to him."

"Thank you, Tony." Joe glanced at Bart with a 'should I tell him?' look. Bart nodded.

"Well, Tony, Bart and I have already been talking. We've had three or four phone conversations already. He let it slip on our last call that you two were going to present the special framed cover to the entire Grayson HR team. Sorry to let you down, but I had to be honest with you."

"Joe, your character is showing," I said. "But now I'm not sure I can trust my boss anymore."

"Better watch him, Tony," grinned Joe. "Your boss is sly like a fox."

The crowd took their seats as the master of ceremonies approached the podium.

Chapter 19

THE FIRST STEP

Close to nine hundred people here, I speculated. A surprisingly diverse mix. My impression of believers in business had just gotten blown out of the water. A Lens Shift for sure.

Then I saw him.

I couldn't help but notice a young man sitting at the next table. Dark hair, dark eyes, a sprinkling of gray showing up around his temples, navy blazer with a crisp blue pinpoint shirt. Everything about him spoke of attention to detail.

But he was obviously very, very uncomfortable. His hands seemed restless. He crossed and uncrossed his legs at the ankle. I noted his eyes darting around the room and his chair pushed back from the table to avoid interaction with others.

What's his story, I wondered. He caught me staring at him, which made him even more uncomfortable. I quickly glanced away.

I wondered if "Mr. Restless" knew about "Joe the Impacter." Did he have any idea that what he was about to hear might change his life, the way he worked, lived, and believed, all for the better?

In an eternal way.

Joe's introduction was well received, including a kind and generous recognition of the Lens Shift article and Spotlight award. Bart was smiling. Everyone gave Joe the warm round of applause he deserved. I even noticed Mr. Restless enthusiastically clapping.

Joe stepped to the podium, thanked the audience for their applause, and then looked directly at me.

"As you know, Lens Shift magazine has chosen Grayson HR as their Spotlight business this year, an incredible honor. I'd like to recognize the writer of that article, Tony Sullivan, here with us today." All eyes in the room turned my way. I braced myself to be publicly berated for the tack I'd taken with the article. Joe had the floor, and this was his opportunity to set the record straight.

"I am proud of Tony for taking this first step in the rest of his life. He's taking time away from his writing career to get to know us, but more important, to get to know himself a little better."

"The first step is always the hardest," Joe continued. "So many of us have taken a similar personal journey, of moving from a passion for success to a passion for significance in our lives. And I know that everyone in this room can relate to my friend, Tony, and the journey he's just now beginning."

Instead of being embarrassed, I found myself feeling encouraged. The subject of a story telling my boss I was taking time away from my career? That had never happened before! Bart gave me a big wink—another first.

"I want to thank Tony personally for having the courage to tell the truth in his article," Joe continued. I felt like slithering under the table. "I think I speak for everyone in this room when I say that I have been on the receiving end of something very unexpected."

Here it came…it was all I could do to keep from clenching my jaw and gripping the table. The room began to swim.

"I have been given a second chance," Joe said after a moment's pause. "I have been forgiven. Now, don't misunderstand me. Forgiveness is not the absence of consequences. Forgiveness is the restoration of a relationship. Tony's article perfectly illustrates the truth that underscores not just my life, but also the lives of everyone in this room. I've made mistakes. We all have. I'm not proud of them. But I am proud to be living proof of the fact that we serve a God of second chances."

The room began coming back into focus, slowly, but I still couldn't look at Joe.

"A few years ago, I made some very poor choices." Joe cleared his throat, and I knew this was as difficult for him to say as it was for me to hear. "Those choices cost me my family. They cost me my business. They cost me the respect and trust of my colleagues and friends. They nearly cost me my life. I'm not proud to say it, but at my worst, my lowest point, I seriously considered ending it all.

"But a man I respected and admired, a lifelong friend of mine, stopped by my house one afternoon when he was in town to speak at a seminar. He didn't call me first, because he knew I wouldn't agree to see him. He just stopped by because he knew I needed to hear what he had to say.

"He reached out to me, a guy no one trusted. It jeopardized his own reputation, but he didn't care about that."

Another pause, and I saw Joe's jaw working as he fought back tears.

"He reminded me that Jesus reached out to people who needed a second chance, and if he were to truly be like Jesus, that was what he needed to do—reach out to me, without judging me or trying to fix me. He knew I needed a friend, an ear, a shoulder, and he was just there to be Jesus to me in the middle of that awful storm in my life.

"I've never forgotten the words my friend shared with me that day," Joe said. "He encouraged me to be willing to let others succeed beyond myself. Said that was the most non-traditional advice he could give me as a businessman, but the best encouragement he could give me as a friend."

Joe was a dynamic storyteller. Through his talk, I learned far more about his personal journey. I could relate to so many of his challenges and struggles, conflicts between work and family, profit and principles, success and significance.

He addressed many of the same issues I struggled with in my own life. Job stress. Career uncertainty. Marital challenges. Health and retirement worries.

A journalist knows how to take good notes. I surprised myself by taking more than five pages of notes on Joe's talk. These were personal notes this time, not for a future Lens Shift story, but for my own future story.

A thunderous round of applause and spontaneous standing ovation ensued as Joe concluded and stepped away from the microphone. It was a great opening session delivered by a great man.

I glanced over to see how Mr. Restless was doing. To my astonishment, he was gone!

Then out of the corner of my eye, I noticed him standing at the bottom of the steps leading to the stage, patiently waiting to say something to Joe.

Looked like he'd taken his first big step.

Frankly, I admitted, I could use some help, some guidance, and some follow-up from someone who'd been in my shoes and could offer wise counsel on what to do next.

Maybe I needed to jump in line, too.

I remembered one phrase that Joe mentioned. He shared how during a particularly tough time in his life, he felt like he was chasing the wind.

That perfectly described how I was feeling. It seemed that I too might be chasing after things that were elusive, assignments and recognitions and possibilities that might be as fruitless as chasing the wind.

Maybe it was time to seek a mentor.

Maybe I should jump in line behind Mr. Restless.

The Impacter Strikes Again!

Chapter 20

THE END...AND THE BEGINNING

As I mentioned earlier, you need to hear this story before hearing mine.

This story, of meeting and befriending Joe Grayson, learning about 2%ers, absorbing the stories of lives transformed by the leadership virtues lived by one man, is just the beginning.

It's the beginning of a journey that has the potential to impact my family and me in a significant and profound way.

It's a journey I have to take.

It's also a journey I want to take.

I've figured this much out: I'm tired of being a wind chaser.

All it takes is a Lens Shift.

About Dr. Jim Harris

Dr. Jim Harris is President of The Jim Harris Group, an international speaking and advising firm dedicated to helping believers in business unleash their unfair advantage in the marketplace. He is the author of *Our Unfair Advantage: Unleash the Power of the Holy Spirit in Your Business* and numerous other award-winning business books.

His clients are a Who's Who in business, including Walmart, IBM, Best Buy, Verizon, Johnson & Johnson, Wells Fargo, Ford, and Walt Disney along with Malcolm Baldrige winners and INC 500 Fast Growth firms.

Dr. Jim is a sought-after speaker at Christian conferences and as a guest preacher. He serves on many Boards of Directors with marketplace and teaching ministries.

The Jim Harris Group
2015 Cameron Drive
Pensacola, FL 32505
850-476-6633
jim@drjimharris.com

Connect with Dr. Jim on...

Web www.DrJimHarris.com

Facebook:/DrJimHarris

Twitter: @DrJimHarris

LinkedIn: DrJimHarris

To purchase copies of *The Impacter* in bulk, please contact High Bridge Books via www.HighBridgeBooks.com/contact.

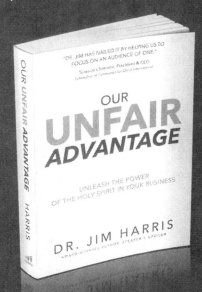

CPSIA information can be obtained
at www.ICGtesting.com
Printed in the USA
FSOW02n0900290815
10310FS

In October 2011, Liam and I were sailing around Mexico on one of our many gay cruises. The ship carried more than two thousand passengers—men and women, but mostly men—for a weeklong party geared 100 percent toward celebrating LGBTQ culture.

For the evening's Halloween bash, a major highlight of the week, I dressed Liam up as the pope, replete with the flowing white robes, sash, and mitre—the tall, peaked ceremonial headdress—a costume I'd picked up for him the previous year in New York. I dressed in a green army jacket with a rainbow flag sewn onto the back.

Hundreds of partiers packed the stage and surrounding outdoor pool area on the ship's top deck, even filling in the upper deck balcony for a better view of the spectacle. All of the lounge chairs had been removed to make room for the party, which featured some of the world's best DJs and a massive laser and light show.

Liam loved to hit the dance floor. Men dressed in all sorts of slutty costumes—cowboys, construction workers, police officers, and some in as little clothing as possible. Every now and again, one of the sexy studs ran up to Liam, kissed his papal ring, and gyrated around him—a dance of such inappropriateness that the rest of the world would cringe to see it. I loved this part of my work, seeing my client join the party not as an observer but fully included. Many members of his older generation dealt with invisibility among a younger crowd, but not on this ship or at this party. We were having a blast.

After a while, Liam headed off to bed. When accompanying clients on these seven-day cruises, I typically take at least one night to myself. Liam had always been good about giving me ample free time, so I took the rest of Halloween night to explore. I found my usual place on the dance floor near a raised hot tub and began dancing around it.

Gazing across the sea of sweaty men, I noticed two guys dancing and checking me out at the same time. I knew immediately I was being cruised, though I didn't give it much thought. But then they came over to chat. They introduced themselves—Todd and Carl had been together for ten years but had an open relationship.

The crowd grew so dense I decided to call it quits and go have some fun in the casino. As I took my seat at the three-card poker table, I noticed Todd walking past the long hall of slot machines. He had close-cropped hair and a beautiful, muscular body—he looked like a tall, svelte, sexy soldier. I smiled to myself. *I need to take this guy out of here before I lose my chance.* He was shy and unassuming, but I knew if I could get him alone, some super-hot sex would ensue.

Gathering up a little courage, I made my move. I stood directly in front of him and said, "Hi, sexy."

"Hello back, sexy."

"Look, I have a few hours off tonight. I would love to connect with you."

No sooner had the words left my mouth than another guy approached from the nearby bar.

"Actually, I already have plans," Todd replied, "but thank you. Maybe another time."

As he waltzed away with his conquest, I felt like a total idiot. About an hour later, he returned to the casino, where I was still losing money playing three-card poker.

He walked up behind me and said, "How about if we meet tomorrow at four in the afternoon?" He told me his cabin number.

"I'll have to ask my client. He's usually pretty good about that, but I don't want to cross any lines with him—he's very important to me. How about if I meet you in the hot tub at the spa just before then, and I will let you know?"

For the rest of the evening, I couldn't get Todd out of my mind. He had an energy about him, and I felt like I had known him forever. I could swear we had met before. He and Carl lived in Palm Springs, California, a place I had only been to a few times for work.

The next day, I broached the subject with Liam. "Would you mind if I took a couple of hours to connect with this guy I met last night?"

"You mean that couple who couldn't take their eyes off you?"

"Well, yes. One of them, anyway."

"Let me guess—the guy with the crew cut."

"Yep." Liam knew me so well.

"Of course you can."

Apparently, Liam had noticed them long before I did and could tell that they were cruising me.

I took off to the spa to meet Todd. When I arrived, he wasn't there. I looked around, trying to be discreet. Steam impaired my view, but I could make out the showers and wooden lounge chairs that surrounded a large, bubbling, twenty-person hot tub. I heard a voice from the roiling water.

"If you're looking for my boyfriend, he isn't here."

I turned around, red-faced, and there was Carl, sitting in the hot tub with a devilish smirk on his face. Carl was beautiful, blond, and blue-eyed, as well as a gentle soul who was deeply bonded to Todd. At first, I thought, *Uh, oh. I have stepped on toes. I'd better scram.* The clock on the wall read 4:00 p.m.

Noticing my glance at the time, Carl said, "It looks like I'm your four o'clock hookup now."

He exited the hot tub fully naked and dripping wet. He walked over and wrapped his body against me. "Todd and I have an agreement—if we both like the same car, we both get to drive it."

I'm as open-minded as anyone, and I wasn't about to turn this man away. Carl was the perfect match for Todd's quiet disposition. Carl seemed fearless with this shift in the power dynamic. I never thought it would be anything more than just a tryst with a hot guy.

Carl and I went to his cabin and went at it for a bit. Soon after we arrived, I heard a tap on the door and looked up to see Todd walk in, feigning innocence.

"I just need to use the restroom," he said. "I'll be out in a second."

Clearly guilty of stealing Todd's hookup, Carl threw on his shorts and scurried out of the room. I found it a bit comical to see them navigating this moment. While the date swap may not have been planned, it certainly seemed expected.

With Carl gone, Todd peered from the bathroom door and began apologizing for interrupting. I just lay there, staring at this man. I was excited. There was something special about him. Although Carl and I had made a clear connection and knew what to expect from one another, Todd was a complete, sexy mystery.

He walked over to the bed and lay next to me. I rolled over on top of him, and we started making out. Before I knew it, we were entangled in a web of pure, passionate, animalistic sex. As a sex worker, I've had my share of kinky, fucked-up, crazy-hot sex, but this was a whole new level of ecstasy. There never seemed to be a disconnect—just one long orgasm. *I never want this to end. I would do anything with this guy. He is a sex machine.*

When we finally finished, we just lay there for a few moments.

"I feel like we've been together before," I said. I'm sure I would have remembered having sex with him, but I just couldn't place him. "I feel like I know you. This feels so strange and yet so familiar."

"No, I don't think so," Todd said, a look of confusion on his face. "If I'd had sex with you, I would never have forgotten." His face was beaming—what we'd experienced was definitely something special.

Todd, Carl, Liam, and I spent a couple of evenings at the dances and dinners together. Liam often nodded with cautious approval as he tried to get to know them. He liked them, but I'm certain he could tell that I was a bit smitten. It's hard for me to control my feelings sometimes.

By this time, Liam and I were like family. I trusted him so much that I told him the details of what had taken place—I held nothing back. He turned out to be understanding and generous with his support. I had been mostly single for about three years—Kurt and I had moved away from the sexual part of our relationship and were now only close friends.

Liam's only concern was for my feelings. He feared that I was being impulsive, which I was. "You could get hurt if you try to embark on an ongoing relationship," he said. "These guys have been together for ten years—you'll always be disposable."

I shared his fear. I also didn't want Liam to feel slighted, so I didn't pursue any more time off.

The boys and I exchanged numbers and stayed in contact after the cruise. A couple of weeks later, I went to Palm Springs to visit them. The three of us had a nice weekend together. They often enjoyed going to the nearby clothing-optional resorts for a weekend, and they invited me to join them. I approached the trip with caution—I reserved my own room—and I tried to contain my emotions, since I had clearly become enamored by the whole situation. At times, I could tell they were sizing me up. Carl was especially inquisitive about my work and travel.

One morning, I woke up early and walked a few doors down to their room. The door was ajar, so I peeked in before knocking. What I saw confirmed all I needed to know about these two. Todd lay in Carl's arms, the two of them loving and affectionate with one another. I'd never witnessed this kind of tenderness before. Their affectionate display told me that after ten years, they were still in love. They hadn't fallen into a rut like many couples in long-term relationships. Their love was palpable.

Not wanting to interrupt, I turned to leave, but Todd called out. "We got you some coffee, David."

I swung open the door to see three cups of coffee from the breakfast room sitting on the nightstand. I crawled into bed next to Todd with Carl on the other side. After a few gentle kisses, Carl and Todd made love to me together. We switched positions often to take turns being together, an insanely beautiful dance that I didn't want to end. Though it was awkward at times, for the most part, I just allowed myself to fully engage and fully participate.

Over the weekend, we had an ongoing chat about triads and what that meant to them. The idea was new to all of us. I